Myth and Memory

My Childhood in World War II Greece

To Michele —
who has such a
lovely daughter —
Katerina

Katerina Katsarka Whitley

APPLECART PRESS

Praise for *Myth and Memory*

As people worldwide long for healing amid political divisiveness and a global pandemic, Katerina Katsarka Whitley, in her artfully written memoir *Myth and Memory*, assures us that adversity can be weathered, that loss can be endured, and that hopeful new days can, and do, dawn anew. Her honest and grace-filled remembrances add insight for all who know the author as a college professor or fellow journalist, and lovingly move all readers toward the light.

—Robert Williams,
Canon for Common Life, Episcopal Diocese of Los Angeles

Whitley's memoir could serve as a cautionary warning against every racist, political, or religious ideology which seeks to impose itself on unwilling recipients.

—William Reader,
Professor Emeritus of Philosophy and Religion,
Central Michigan University

In *Myth and Memory* Katerina Katsarka Whitley not only creates a memoir of intense emotional power, drawing on deep memories that well up from her earliest childhood in Thessaloniki, Greece during the Nazi occupation up to her first year of college in North Carolina, but also performs an act of filial piety, creating portraits of her parents (and grandparents) that testify to her love of family, and of her home country. She sees and records for us the torturous political history of Greece in the WWII war years, and presents her slow blossoming as a girl and then young woman in a prose that is lean, precise, evocative and lyrical.

—David Gullette,
Founding Editor of Fenway Press and Literary Director of
the Poets' Theatre in Boston

Also by Katerina Katsarka Whitley

Speaking for Ourselves: Voices of Biblical Women

Seeing for Ourselves: Biblical Women Who Met Jesus

Walking the Way of Sorrows: Stations of the Cross

Waiting for the Wonder: Voices of Advent

Light to the Darkness: Lessons and Carols, Public and Private

A New Love, a novel of the First Century

*Around a Greek Table, Recipes and Stories Arranged
According to the Liturgical Seasons of the Eastern Church*

Book design by Brenda Klinger
Cover design by Brenda Klinger
Copyediting by Jennifer Hanshaw Hackett
Proofreading by Amy Wagner

Printed in the United States of America
ISBN 978-0-578-76291-3
10 9 8 7 6 5 4 3 2 1
First Edition

In memory of my father and my mother,
with love

In a Greek folk costume, on a national holiday, the author, twelve years of age. A formal picture in a studio was a must those days.

Contents

Pronunciation of Greek Names

About the title: Myth derives from the Greek *mythos*—a word weighted by multiple meanings and riches. My students used to say, "A myth is a fairytale," and I would spend the rest of the class explaining why myth is so much more and so much truer: that our world is so full of mystery that only a story, a myth, can make sense of it; that life hides so many terrors and so much that is unknowable that the ancients made sense of it by creating and telling stories; and that because we do not have the words to explain all the mystery, wonder, and terror, only a myth will do. And what of memory? Why do we remember—see—events of tragedy and fear more than those of joy? Only a story can capture those short, vivid memories, so that in the telling they become bearable. The Greeks knew how to tell stories; we retell them as the myths that never die.

Proper names: It's always a problem to translate Greek place names and people's names. In English, the Latin ending *us* has been adopted, rather than the Greek *os* for masculine nouns. For example, the Greek mountain ranges, Ólympos and Pindos, referred to in this memoir, are known as Mt. Olympus and Mt. Pindus, but I prefer the Greek endings for such names. Many place names end with the Greek word for city *polis,* which becomes –ople in English, as in Adrianoupolis/Adrianople, Constantinoupolis/Constantinople. I use the English spelling for these two cities because of historic familiarity and for ease in understanding. One problematic place name for historic reasons and because of cultural appropriation is *Macedonia.* The northern province of Greece has always been Makedonía, not to be confused with the now-Slavic

North Macedonia, whose name is a contrived solution after many arguments between the two countries. To avoid ethnic confusion, I use the Greek spelling Makedonía throughout this memoir.

People's names seem difficult to English speakers because the Greek language is inflective—that means it changes endings according to gender and case. So the masculine name Vassilis becomes Vassili in the vocative—when one is being addressed; then, the final "s" is dropped. In this memoir, when I call my father I say, "Babá," but when he is the subject of the sentence, the word becomes Babás. The same usage applies to the accusative (objective) case.

Accents are the ones that always get transposed in English. A rule of thumb is that most proper names in Greek accent the penultimate—the next-to-last—syllable. Thus, Persephóne, Katerína, Dorítsa, and so on. Throughout this memoir I try to stay faithful to these sounds and accents. Whenever you see Greek names, drop down the accent one syllable, and you will be right. Thus, Socrátes, Euripídes, Aristotéles, Thucydídes, Athéna, have accents in the penultimate.

Dates: In Greek, as in most European languages, the day comes first, then the month, followed by the year. Thus, 28 October 1940, the vital date in this Anamnesis. I follow this pattern throughout.

MAP   11

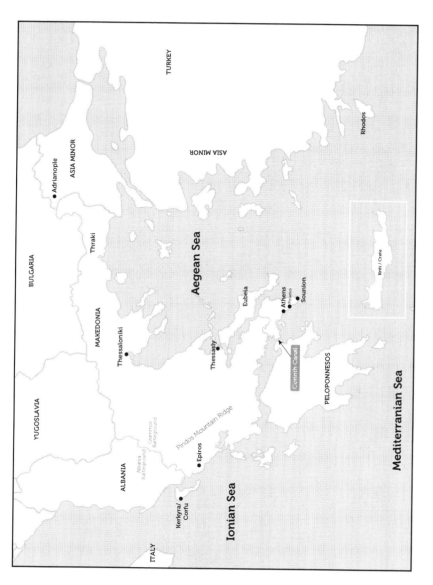

A map of Greece and bordering countries as it was in 1940, showing only the places mentioned in the memoir. Credit: Brenda Klinger.

The Pindos woman, carrying battle provisions, is part of the narrative of the war with the Italians. Author's photo.

Prologue: The Twentieth Century

> Wherever I travel
> Greece wounds me.
>
> —G. Seferis, *"In the Manner of G. S."*

To the Greeks who know their history, 28 October 1940, has entered the realm of ancient myths. The Greek army's unexpected victory over Mussolini's Italians was praised throughout an astounded world. But that victory was quickly ignored. Even a journalist of William L. Shirer's fame dismissed the little country with two short mentions in his book *The Nightmare Years.* "Occupation of Albania would give the Duce a springboard against Greece and Yugoslavia. And a cheap victory." It was an extremely costly defeat for the ridiculous Duce. Later, in passing, Shirer includes this throwaway line: "Mussolini, not to be outdone by Hitler, had invaded a new country, Greece, on October 28." And that's it, in a book that spans a decade and covers more than six hundred pages.

In 1940, Greece was in the fourth year of a dictatorship under a short, professorial, German-educated general named Ioannis Metaxas. He had done away with democracy and had been exceptionally harsh on Communists, aligning himself with an ambitious but clueless king, George II, who boasted not a drop of Greek blood. Yet, near dawn on 28 October, when the Italian ambassador rang the prime minister's residence in the elegant Athens suburb of Kifissia to hand Metaxas an ultimatum by Mussolini, Metaxas simply said,

"C'est la guerre."[1] Though sympathetic to the Fascists, he knew the passion of the Greeks for their land and for freedom and opted for war rather than allowing the arrogant Mussolini to humiliate his courageous little country. Greek folklore has repeated this event by changing "C'est la guerre" to *"oxi"* (*"no!"*). From then on, that date, 28 October, has become a national holiday.

Now, more than seventy years later, the number of those of us who remember is dwindling fast. We who have those scant but frightful childhood images of WWII etched in our brains will soon be gone. The rest remember the stories as told and written. Their images are painted by others. Ours are our own.

28 OCTOBER 1940

The date entered Greek lore together with our historical passion and all the fervor of a nation that remembers old glories in order to forget the painful present. The old glories go back to pre-Christian centuries. Names of city-states and of excavated ruins dwell in the memory and in the scholarly books of all nations; they are our heritage, we think, all those long-lost civilizations: Minoan, Mycenaean, Homeric, and the fifth-century classical—the Golden Age—which ushered in Western civilization.

The thousand years of Byzantium are claimed by the Greeks as their own, until the Greek-speaking world's dark ages arrived—the four centuries of Ottoman occupation. Greece, together with Byzantium, was forgotten. At last, though, on 25 March 1821, the sleeping country woke up and, despite the long darkness, remembered the light and fought to emerge into independence.

All of this covers a long, long span of time—some eras of pride and others of shame. Yet, more than a century after Greece achieved

---

[1] "That's war."

independence, on 28 October 1940, a new triumph was born, a myth resurrected. Salamis, Marathon, and Thermopylae came alive again, and we, in Greek Makedonía, newly liberated, reclaimed Alexander the Great. To the famous places of Athenian, Spartan, and Makedonian memorials would be added the name of Pindos and Epiros, the forbidding western mountain range and the wildest province of Greece, together with towns in Albania bearing Greek names reclaimed for the motherland—Argyrókastro, Korytsá, Ayioi Saránta. And the name of Mussolini, the preposterous invader, would become the ultimate ridicule, despite the sorrow he caused.

This is our modern-day myth, and it is based on historic facts: on that 28 October 1940, tiny Greece refused passage to Italy, with its powerful Axis connection, and denied entrance to the bloated Mussolini, who fancied himself a new Caesar. He demanded an easy passage through our land as though we did not matter; we said *oxi*, *no*, and emerged as the first country to defeat an Axis power. Why has that startling victory been ignored by history books? Why is the role of Greece in WWII passed over in the retelling of the terrible narratives of that war? In writing my memories, I am attempting to correct this evasion.

The Greek army, small and roughly clad, defeated the well-dressed and newly armed Italians on the snowy crags of Pindos and in the hostile hovels and mountains of Albania—despite Italy's vastly superior air power, numbers, and equipment. The Hellenes' courage astonished a world that groveled in defeat after the Axis powers' rapid victories in most of the much larger European countries. The blitzkrieg employed by the Nazis and the paralyzing fear that gripped even great France made the Axis appear unbeatable. Yet, the first victory against them was achieved by the poor Greek soldiers trudging on the frozen ranges of our western mountains and of Albania, in boots that let the ice water seep through. Among them, my reluctant father and his brothers. When Hitler, summoned by an embarrassed Mussolini, sent his terrible armies south a few months later, these same soldiers would return to the cities and the villages in bug-infested rags, their feet frostbitten, many with legs amputated on the battlefield under conditions reminiscent of the Great War, a generation earlier. In the years following the victory and the brief months of glory, many of these soldiers would have to beg for bread in the streets of our cities. This shame would never leave us.

And what of the rest, those who stayed behind? This is what I remember.

That Fateful Afternoon

Memoir writing is very challenging. It can be done
in many different ways. For me, I prefer following the
operation of memory itself. We don't remember in a linear
sense. We have a selection of slides in the mind, as it were,
and any of those can pop out of the mind. In any hour you
could think of something that happened as a child, twenty
years ago or yesterday. Memoir should reflect that. . . .
Every life is interesting and every way of writing about it
would be interesting.

— Penelope Lively

We are standing at the open front window, looking
up at the sky. An airplane is flying above, my first sight
of one, and I marvel at its size. "Look, look, Dorítsa. It's
tiny. It looks like a bird." And my sister, wiser by four
years, responds: "But it's really very large. As large as that
building," and she points across to the squat structure
that houses the Turkish baths. Distracted, I watch the
women who emerge from the hamam carrying towels
and bags of clothes. The soapy steam of the baths drifts
across the street as I try to visualize an airplane that large,
but I fail. And then a new sound makes me forget the
plane. A rousing song, a trumpet and a drum, and young
feet marching to their rhythm. The girls, dressed in white

and blue, are a few years older than my sister. They start from uphill coming toward us, in orderly lines, proud in their uniforms. Now more windows open up, balcony shutters clatter, some cheering accompanies the girls, but underneath it all is a kind of murmur, a disapproval. The girls continue to march. Their lives and ours will change radically, as early as tomorrow.

꧇ ꧇ ꧇

Later I would learn that Hitler's youth corps enthusiasms had traveled south to our own dictator, Metaxas, who adored the law and order of the Fascists. The young, organized into EON, the Greek equivalent of Nazi Youth, had to be trained early for this kind of obedience. Among us, however, the fervor would pass into oblivion; among the German youth it would cause destruction for them and for most of Europe.

꧇ ꧇ ꧇

Again we are at the open window, but this time my mother sits with her back to it. The afternoon light of that fateful October day falls on her wet hair and on the tiny infant she is holding in her arms. Her gray-green eyes are troubled. My older sister and brother stop what they are doing and inch closer to her. I do the same, though, at less than four years of age, I sense more than I understand. Mammá is listening to our dad (Babás) who has just returned from somewhere in the city, a place that has agitated him, and all these adult emotions rush toward us so powerfully that, without being told, we pause in quiet to listen. Tears roll down my cheeks and fall on my red dress. "Babá, I don't like you in that *soldiering*. Go take it off and put on your clothes." His voice, sad, worried, stays with me as he says to my mother: "They're calling everyone up, Persephóne. I couldn't change their minds."

"But you have four children!" she cries and her fear enters me, so I turn from one to the other knowing that what is happening is not good. The word *pólemos*, war, is repeated, together with longer words like "general mobilization." The baby cries. My mother's eyes keep producing those fat tears that run silently down her cheeks.

My parents had thought that this fourth child would save them from separation, since it had been announced that they were not calling up fathers with more than three children. But everything changed on 28 October 1940.

TOWARD THE FRONT

My father had lived through wars and was well aware of both the courage of the Greeks and the perfidy of many among them, especially of those in the ruling class. He was steeped in the history of the nation and marveled at the accomplishments of his fellow Greeks, but he was also clear-eyed regarding the passions, arrogance, and greed that plunged the nation into schism and misery. Like most Greeks who arrived in the mainland from Asia Minor, he was a Venizelist, a follower of the one great statesman Greece produced in modern times. Eleftherios Venizelos was revered by all true democrats in the nation; the rest were royalists and nationalists, a laughable state of being in the land that gave the world the definition of democracy.

The story of how democratic Greece became a monarchy owes its origins to the interference of the so-called Great Powers.

The Greek royal family was not Greek. A Bavarian royal was imposed on liberated Greece after the 1821 War of Independence against the Ottoman Empire by England, France, Russia, and Prussia, the Great Powers that have played through countless decades a dishonorable game with our poor but strategically located land.

Dad told us later that when they first called up his age group he was convinced that they would not order him to the front. He showed his papers to the officer in charge, who became incensed at the suggestion that four children would excuse him from going to battle. "Take him and dress him," he ordered one of the sergeants, so when Dad returned to us, he looked different. It was he who remembered my red dress and the funny words I created as I learned to speak in long sentences. At the beginning, he managed to escape the barracks three nights in a row, to sleep at home, but on the fourth day the trains had started loading the new troops, moving them closer to the western mountains, to the front, and he was gone. Over the months he kept remembering the words of my brother as he stood at the door that last day, pleading: "Don't be late tonight, Babá. Come home early." It would be nearly six months before we saw him again.

Our mother reacted in despair. Forbidden by the doctor to nurse her baby, she was bereft. She would pour milk into a small pot to boil it, since it was brought to us straight from the cows in the country, unpasteurized. With three other children underfoot she would forget and invariably the milk would scorch. The smell of burnt milk remains my memory of that apartment.

It was on the first floor, without a balcony, and I remember it as dark. There is only the image of that large window and the front stoop where we children played. After the call-up, our grandparents came to live with us because, out of their five sons, our father's family had the greatest need. One of the aunts, together with her little boy, also joined our household. All of my grandfather's five sons had been called up, and only the youngest, who was a dentist and an army major, was allowed to stay in the city. My grandfather, a man of unshakable faith, was convinced that God would spare his sons. He prayed that not one of them would be forced to kill another human being, and his prayers were answered. All four were assigned to positions behind the fighting lines.

We children played in the street, our games war-centered. The first three days of November brought with them the Italian air force. Their planes, painted with the Hellenic colors of blue and white to deceive the populace, caused much harm to handsome buildings near the waterfront and to the people who stopped to gaze on them thinking they belonged to the Greek air force. The new month entered our world with the howl of sirens, my most persistent acoustic memory of those days. Our boy cousins were visiting and we were outside, as usual. There were now stacked rocks covering basement windows—something new in the neighborhood—so we tried to climb on them, pretending we were running from the bombs when sirens started their ominous crescendo and we, confused, didn't know what to do.

The real interfered with the imagined. The cries of our mothers calling our names brought us to our senses, and we ran together to the shelter. We were laughing, but we were afraid. Our city, Thessaloniki, was bombed that day and the electric station very close to our neighborhood suffered a direct hit. Bomb shelters were few and those in the basements were in dire condition.

My memories of subsequent bombings hover over scant images. In that dark apartment, crowded with five little children, two young mothers, and two grandparents who seemed aged but were only in their fifties, we spent our days and nights waiting for the war to end, for Daddy to return, and for our lives to resume their ordinary but oh, so loved, routine. But we were little children and we had each other for our simple games that centered not on toys but on whatever we could imagine.

The remembered routine seems to be happening in an unending present when I pause to recall those months.

The howl of the sirens startles us. It's a visceral sound that shakes the whole body. Mammá, fragile and nervous, places a small pot of milk on the stove for the baby who, the moment the sirens begin their howl, starts her own lusty wailing. How does such a large sound emerge from a tiny body? The grown-ups gather us for the descent to the shelter next door, since our building lacks its own basement. We hate the place. It is damp, nasty, and gloomy, hostile with arguments and fear. We would much rather stay home. When Mammá arrives carrying the baby, the quarrel-ling makes us acutely uncomfortable. The baby does not stop her crying and the neighbors complain that the enemy will hear it and bomb us directly. My aunt, with the preposterous name of Stavroforia (Crusade), is mouthy; she asks them: "Do you think the Italians up in their noisy planes are going to hear a little baby down here and bomb us? Have you lost your minds?" We huddle together, embarrassed and worried about what it all means.

With immense relief we hear the all-clear and emerge from the darkness and the smell of fear into the light of the deserted street. Soon windows and doors open and people appear as if arousing from a bad dream. What has been hit? This is the prevailing question. Relief rains over everyone: we have escaped; we are still alive and not injured. The knowledge quickens people's steps, and a few courageous voices are raised together with fists shaking toward the sky. "Those stupid *makaronádhes,* that *vlaka* Moussolini, may the devil take him."

By the second day in November, the Greek army had pushed the Italians out of our soil and into Albania. Thessaloniki, our northern city, was delirious with victory. The conversations centered on the courage of the Greek army at the front. The word in Greek is *méto-po,* which up to then I had known only as "forehead." So this was the forehead of Hellás, of our country, the one with the feminine name, the motherland depicted as a Greek goddess. We were in the body of Greece, but our daddy was at her forehead. What was he doing there? It was impossible—no, preposterous—to imagine him holding a gun.

Grateful to have returned home from the war, the Katsarka family enjoyed being together; here, a welcome visit to the countryside.

The Reluctant Soldier

> Boys, Children of Greece,
> You who are fighting hard on the mountains,
> We are praying to the sweet Virgin for your return.
>
> —from one of Sophia Vembo's
> most popular wartime songs.
>
> —Author's translation

While those of us left behind in Thessaloniki hid from the Italian air raids and tried to survive without husbands and fathers, a different, relentless struggle for survival was taking place west and north of us, in the fertile plain of western Makedonía, that beautiful northern part of Greece ignored by Athens and the Greek government in favor of the more famous province of Attica. The following scenes are gleaned from my father's notes. At thirty-seven years of age, with four little children and a fragile wife left behind, he was an exceptionally reluctant warrior. The word "soldier" did not fit him, and to his credit he never pretended otherwise, nor did he deny his aversion to war. But I would not call him a pacifist.

Dad had seen what war does to families, to mothers and children left behind. In the first two decades of his life he had witnessed enough wars to last many lifetimes.

He was born in Adrianople—that was the city's Greek name, changed to the Turkish Edirne in the 1930s. It lies in eastern Thraki, the ancient Thrace, near the borders of Greece, Turkey, and

Bulgaria—a dangerous combination at a strategic location. It's almost inevitable with Greek names that I delve into their etymology because within the secrets of these words lies history and—since this is Greece—mythology.

Ancient myth tells us that Orestes, he of the terrible, doomed house of Atreus—remember, Agamemnon was his father—landed in Adrianople after he killed his murderous mother, Clytemnestra. So the city at first was named Oresteia, and later, at the beginning of the second century, the Roman emperor Hadrian, a lover of all things Greek (including a beautiful boy named Antinoos), embellished the city and named it after himself: Hadrian's City. In Greek, his name is *Adrianos,* which in the possessive and combined with *polis,* becomes Adrianou-polis. The Western Europeans, who delighted in screwing up Greek names, called it Adrianople.

My father loved his birthplace and remembered every detail of it as if someone had drawn it on his brain with indelible ink. It seemed natural to hear him describe it until I grew up and realized how remarkable that nearly photographic memory was. He had left the city forever at eleven years of age, yet, when his words painted a picture of the verdant edges of the rivers I could hear and almost feel the flow of the water. The city was built on the confluence of three rivers, Toundja, Arda, and Maritza, and boasted the most beautiful mosques and those huge, domed markets of the Ottoman world, which the Greeks have always called *agora* and the Arabs, *souk.*

When my father was in the second grade, he was told at school that his city was multicultural, something he experienced every day in his walks around the neighborhoods. It's only the numbers of the various nationalities that he learned at school: their characteristics, customs, and dress were already familiar to him. In that first decade of the twentieth century, of the eighty thousand inhabitants of Adrianople, twenty-two thousand were Greeks; thirty thousand, Turks; ten thousand, Bulgarians; four thousand, Armenians; and twelve thousand were Jews. The rest, mostly Europeans, lumped together as Franks, ran the banks and the railroad.

The center of the city was called Kastro, the Castle, surrounded by six suburbs, each with its own distinct population and color. The richest one, Kara-agatz, was the enclave of Europeans, and I could picture easily and with envy their fancy villas and flowering gardens. But the suburb that fascinated me, bringing a thrill, a frisson of adventure, was the one that housed the poorest, criminal portion of the Greek population, the precursors of gangs, for they consisted of unruly young men. They wore clothes woven on the loom, and around their middle they wrapped their famous red *zonas*. The cloth of these belts was fifteen meters in length and two palms in width, as Daddy described it. They bulged in the front. Inside those folds they hid their two-edged knives, *kama*, a sack of tobacco with cigarette papers, and who knows what else. Every morning, seated outside the cafés of their neighborhoods, they would start the ritual of rolling cigarettes. Instead of matches, they used flint to light them. Lazy people have a lot of time to perform minor activities. Their foaming, heavy-sweet coffee was served in mugs without handles.

The rest of the Greek inhabitants, embarrassed by the manners of these young men, formed a progressive society that offered free lectures and festivals in order to bring the gangs into the civilized fold of the city. They made an effort to disabuse gang members of their "Asiatic barbarism," as my father put it sixty-four years later. He knew all this because his beloved uncle, a sweet man who smiled and laughed easily, who also wore the red *zona* and held the ubiquitous *komboloï*, worry beads, lived in this same Ildirim, where no foreigner would ever dare to enter. These were the pictures absorbed by a little boy who could roam the streets with his brother without any fear of being hurt.

Each of the other four suburbs, named and described in fine detail by my father, had its own color and customs, and he never forgot their idiosyncrasies. In this polyethnic city of beautiful mosques, markets, and graceful bridges, the little boy was enveloped by love of family and the excitement of different cultures but also by the harsh dangers and deprivations of war. It was in this idyllic city that he lived through the two Balkan Wars, where he saw a man hanging from a tree and the bloated body of another floating down the river. There, his family lived through the famous siege of Adrianople and its accompanying famine. Those events shaped his lifelong horror of war.

Later, in 1922, the most terrible year for the Greek army, the year they were routed in the "great catastrophe" and lost Smyrna and everything they had gained in Asia Minor after World War I, he was drafted to fulfill his military duty. Vassilis Katsarkas, an innocent in the ways of the world, entered into an alien territory where both language and training were brutal; he hated every moment of it. He had lived such an isolated, protected life in the cocoon of a large, loving family, under the guidance of a strong father and a community of puritanical Protestants who seemed to have drawn a circle around themselves that kept them from contact with the rest of the world. And now, suddenly, he was thrust in with young men who used profanity he had never heard, who were ready to fight among themselves, and who made fun of everything that he held sacred. How would he endure the remaining two years?

One morning, early in his basic training, while standing in the inspection line, he heard a voice calling out: "Everyone who speaks English, French, or German, step forward." Vassilis knew enough English and Turkish to converse comfortably and thought, *What do I have to lose?* He stepped forward and his life changed immediately.

He no longer had to sleep on the freezing floor or to exercise in harsh conditions. He became a translator/interpreter among Greeks, Brits, and Turks. So he never suffered the hardships of basic training, and he never learned how to hold and fire a gun. And now, thirty-seven years old, he found himself at the front, untrained, in a real, justified, defensive war, so he was given charge of a mule.

In 1940, as a muleteer in the mountain artillery, he would not be called on to fight. His job was to load and unload the mule, to care for it, and lead it on to the destination of each marching day. The mules were indispensable in a war fought in the mountains by an army that lacked tanks. Without this humble animal, the Greek army, specifically the artillery, could not have been equipped. Their contribution was enormous and they deserve a paean written just for them.

My father respected his faithful animal, which probably saved his life. He remembered the early days of the endless trudging:

> The trains are full but they cannot carry us far. The rail lines end and the rest of the push to the front will be on foot. We march only at night, we, the unlucky replacement troops from Thessaloniki. The army at the front is already exhausted. As we leave the city and its suburbs behind, we find ourselves in open terrain, in the countryside, vulnerable to attacks from the air. The Italians have a brand-new air force and ours is so limited, the airplanes so old, that despite the pilots' brilliance and exceptional courage, they cannot offer us any support. Soon, however, to our relief and perverse amusement, we discover that the Italians are not smart flyers and their bombing is far from accurate.

After marching all night, we stop to rest in deserted villages with their abandoned huts and homes. Where have the inhabitants gone? We take over their homes, eat the cabbages that are left in the fields, and thank these unknown benefactors. At such times I look around me and think: If the Italian planes come now, they will destroy most of us. But on sunny days, when a whole army gathers out in the open, the Italians do not come. We are glad, but the worry is like a worm in my gut: Are they bombing the city instead? It's impossible to stop thinking of my loved ones, so I spend my hours of rest writing letters.

Soon the plains of Makedonía give way to the mountainous terrain of Western Greece, and our trudging becomes all the more difficult. The night marches are horrific. The struggle to stay awake is agonizing. It is so cold that our legs and feet are numb.

The mountain paths are extremely narrow, but now it's worse: we are on goat tracks. Sharp, high crags on the left, open gorges and ravines on the right, gaping dark like Hades in the moonless, snowy nights. We muleteers start out fresh and ready in the early dark only to be overtaken by the unbearable, urgent need for sleep around two in the morning. The desire for sleep is so intense that it grips the chest like physical pain. The sergeant up ahead of the line calls out the order that is repeated down the single-file: "Men, drop your reins and let the mules lead you. Don't try to force them. They know the way." We had been warned that if the mule slipped and we still held on to the reins, we too would slide with the animal down the frozen crevasse. So we trust the mules ahead of us to lead us in the dark, these suddenly precious, sure-footed animals that not only find the way but carry the war's burden on their backs. We men are loaded with as heavy a pack as our back can endure, but it is the mules that carry the disassembled, heavy machine gun parts. Without them, the war cannot be fought.

At the first light, great relief would flood the men. Then they and their poor animals could rest. The glory of the Greeks' improbable courage and the carnage of fighting take a back seat as I read my father's notes. Winning against the invading Italians depends on what most writers ignore. The first duty of these trudging soldiers is to take care of the mule in their charge: unload, wipe down, wash, brush. "This mule is much more important to this war than I am," Dad would jot down. After the animals were settled, the exhausted men would try to find a place to rest, to hide from the Italian air force, to sleep and, above all, to write letters home. My father, unlike most Greeks, was quite fair. His skin was very light and thin, with that unfortunate epidermis that blisters easily. During the early marches, his greatest misery was caused by the enormous blisters inside the inadequate boots. Woolen socks from home were the most welcome gift of all.

An observant man, his impressions of men and events are vivid in Dad's letters. As they approach the Greco-Albanian border, they meet returning soldiers who, exhausted from a month's constant battles, are making their way to Epiros. "Courage, boys!" they cry to the newcomers. "We have beaten them. They're running like hares and are giving themselves up. In a little while we will throw them to the sea." The fresh troops take heart even though now they are crossing the border to an alien land. They reach Albanian villages. In his letters Dad describes their miserable state, the emptiness of their hovels after two armies have marched through. Where have the people gone? In one hut, he meets with an old man, an Albanian peasant who had not escaped. The man speaks Turkish, so they spend the night talking to each other and Dad writes pages and pages of the old man's story-telling, of the construction of their huts, of the villagers' suffering and the necessity of emigration.

When the troops stop in no-man's land, he watches the medics carrying the wounded and hears their moans of pain. The medics sing a mournful song, a dialogue between Charon and the dying. "Let me stay, let me stay, Charon. What will happen to my wife and children?" Reminiscent of Homer, the sad keening echoes through the eons of man's greatest sin and stupidity—war.

Looking at History

Oh traveler, announce to the Spartans that here we
lie, obedient to their will.

—Simonides, on the sacrifice of the three hundred
Spartans at Thermopylae.

—Author's Translation

The Greco-Italian war was the defining event of the Greek generation that grew up in the first half of the twentieth century. Diaries,
journals, and books written about those six months are filled with
pride and the initial sweet smell of victory. It was truly the kind of
event that echoed the triumph of the ancient Athenians and Spartans against the hordes of Xerxes: a small group of dedicated men,
trained by intelligent officers, fighting against a huge army of well-
equipped but unmotivated men. The immense contribution of the
women of Epiros who climbed through knee-deep snows, carrying
supplies on their backs to the soldiers on the steep mountainsides,
echoed the courage of the Spartan mothers who long ago had sent
their sons to battle with the cry, *"I tan, i epi tas."* (Return either *with*
your shield—victorious—or *on* it—dead.) The women of Epiros and
of the Pindos mountains carried ammunition and food supplies on
their backs, walking for eighteen uninterrupted hours, dressed in
inadequate clothing and shod in homemade shoes. On their return,
they carried the wounded to hospitals. This is the stuff of myths, but

the reality of the women's contribution is more impressive than the mightiest mythology.

The madness of Mussolini—his arrogance and conviction of victory—had not reached down to the ordinary Italian soldier. Metaxas, though a dictator enamored of Fascism, had read the Greek people with a remarkable accuracy when he decided on war instead of capitulation. Eyewitness reports describe the joy and verve of the Greek soldiers as they marched to meet the Italians. They fought for their beloved land and they were victorious, to the astonishment of the world watching with glee the first defeat of an Axis power. The ancient Greeks, like the legendary Odysseus, had seen the goddess Athena, fully armed, fighting alongside them. The soldiers of 1940 described how they felt the presence of an armed Virgin Mary next to them. The power of myth endures.

This war lasted for six months. The Italians were pushed away from Greek soil, unable to break through the stubborn Greek defenses. In January, Metaxas died and Greece lost a strategic mind. Mussolini, desperate for victory, visited his demoralized troops as young Italians were dying in melting snows and mud. The Greeks were not budging.

But when the almond trees started blossoming in February, the first hint in Greece that spring is arriving, rumors drifted to the south that the Germans, despite Hitler's reluctance to get involved in the Balkans, were preparing to march through Yugoslavia into Greece. Hitler, eager to invade Russia, had refused to send his armies to the Balkans, but he also feared that the British would send help to the Greeks, thus cutting off his supply lines to North Africa. British soldiers sent to assist the Greek fighting men, though courageous, proved to be inadequate, their masters in London sending confusing orders. Hitler, unwilling to be humiliated further by the defeat of his main Axis ally, decided to come to the aid of the bloated Duce.

The heart breaking beauty of April in Greece arrived together with the news that the German *blitzkrieg* to the south had begun.

In late March, on the Albanian front, the soldiers had felt lost. Rumors of capitulation and surrender spread; in the northeast, along the Yugoslav/Bulgarian border, the Metaxas Line, an impressive chain of twenty-one fortifications, held, but its improbably courageous defenders were few—too few—against the German hordes, since most of the Greek army was still in the northwest. The hated Bulgarians, now allied with the Germans, were ready to invade from the northeast. So courageous were the defenders at the Metaxas Line that even the renowned German field marshal, General Wilhelm List, together with his officers and soldiers, had nothing but admiration for the way the Greeks fought. He ordered that Greek soldiers not be taken prisoner—they could retreat with their banners but not their weapons.

There was no guidance arriving from Athens to the courageous men who fought on the two fronts. The man who succeeded Metaxas as prime minister committed suicide. The government, lacking direction, lost control of the armed forces, while individual generals made their own decisions. One of them, George Tsolakoglou, took it upon himself to surrender to the invading German army, even though the commander-in-chief, Alexander Papagos, was determined to resist to the end. Tsolakoglou claimed that he saved the Greek army by signing the surrender, but offered himself as the first collaborationist Greek prime minister to Hitler. At the western front, the brilliant officers who had defeated Mussolini were filled with bitterness. This became exacerbated when the now emboldened Italians demanded that Greece should surrender to them, not to the Germans, who also despised the Italians. Greek soldiers, embittered, hurt, and humiliated started drifting toward their homes. My father reported that at first their retreat was orderly, but without leadership from Athens, the fields rampant with defeatist rumors, the orderly retreat collapsed. Those who refused to surrender took to the mountains, most of them to stay there as resisters throughout the occupation. Among the lost soldiers was my father, eager to return home to his wife and children. All kinds of rumors were circulating—that the Germans would kill them if they found them armed, that even their army uniforms put them in danger. So, many of them abandoned everything, even their good army blankets, to rapacious peasants. On the way, they saw the now-rescued Italians still begging to be allowed to surrender themselves to the Greeks. Meanwhile, an exhausted German army was marching south, ignoring the Greek soldiers who just weeks before had been triumphant. The Germans entered Greece hungry and without supplies, and the whole country paid dearly for this lack when the proud Nazis, acting like bandits, stripped the land of all that was valuable.

The Greeks soon realized that the Italian enemy they had defeated and utterly despised would now lord it over them, since Italy and Germany were allies. The megalomaniac Mussolini kept demanding that the Greek generals surrender to the Italians, an unbearable humiliation. The remaining Greek army, together with New Zealanders, Australians, and Brits, continued to fight as they retreated to the Peloponnesos and, when lucky, to Crete. However, entire infantry companies of Greeks, especially those from the island of Crete, were not able to return home. Proud, victorious fighters became homeless, dispirited drifters.

The enemy raised its despised swastika on our sacred rock, the Acropolis, on 27 April 1941. The officers among them—those who had had a classical education—boasted that their Aryan race was ready to appreciate the glories and contributions of ancient Greece. Their propaganda insisted that they would respect the Greeks.

But after taking dozens of pictures on the Acropolis, they quickly forgot all promises of acting with civility. Soon Hitler, who was planning to invade Russia and was reluctant to commit many troops to Greece, was forced to send them across the Aegean to the proud island of Crete. Thousands upon thousands of German paratroopers descended from the sky, many of them to be massacred by retreating Greek and British soldiers and by Cretans wielding any tool they could find, even iron rakes. The destruction of the German army was so great that Hitler declared that never again would he invade with paratroopers. But the German air force was unstoppable and the island's airports were quickly destroyed and Allied planes obliterated. The British continued to retreat to the southern shores of the island to be rescued by boats and taken to Cairo. With them went the king of Greece and the Greek government, who lived lives of comfort and indifference in Cairo while the people of Greece suffered beyond measure. Those Brits who remained on the island were hidden by the Cretans even though, if discovered, this act of mercy would mean death for them and their families. In the wild mountains of the legendary island, a few remaining Allied troops fought together with the intrepid islanders who were familiar, throughout many centuries, with war and with survival.

By 21 May the Germans controlled all of Greece, including Crete, but their own garrisons remained chiefly in Thessaloniki and in central Athens. The rest of the country was under the control of the hated Italians. Northeastern Greece was given to brutal Bulgarian garrisons, the worst insult of all. And so, for us in Thessaloniki, the years of occupation, of *Katohí*, began in April 1941.

The Return

And even more honor is due to them
when they foresee (as many do foresee)
that in the end Ephialtis will make his appearance,
that the Medes will break through after all.

— C. P. Cavafy, *Thermopylae*

Spring arrived not with joy but with gloom. We had waited through that first winter of the war, veering from terror to joy, from fear to victory. From November on the newspapers and our songs proclaimed that we were great again. Little Greece had beaten the pants off the arrogant, ridiculous buffoon, Mussolini, who thought himself the reincarnation of Julius Caesar. November, December, January, February, March passed, a winter made terrible in Albania, on the snow-covered Pindos mountains, and in our cities, empty of men and food. But our soldiers had persisted and, recalling other great battles in our long, long history, gave us back our damaged pride. Little Greece was the only victorious country against the barbarians of the Axis powers who had toppled Czechoslovakia, Poland, Belgium, and even France without significant opposition and without stopping to rest.

Sophia Vembo's deep contralto sang of victory over the city's loudspeakers. She sang in the plaintive minor key of Greek music, calling the men *paidiá*, "children," the affectionate word universally used by Greeks for those they love, no matter their age. She sang of the ridiculous Mussolini and his underlings and their response to the cry

Aéra. Why this word, which means "air" or "wind" in Greek, made the Italians tremble with fear is a mystery. On the snowy crags of Albania, the Greek soldiers would jump up yelling *Aéra!*, and the terrified Italians would drop their weapons, raise their arms, and surrender. It was heady stuff.

But now, as April was approaching and the Greek countryside was blooming with the red of the *paparounes* (poppies) and the white-gold of *margarites* (daisies), and the herbs filled the air with the aroma that invades the Greek senses, word reached us that the monster known as *blitzkrieg* was rushing south. The king and his entourage, together with the Greek government, were already in the safety of exile in Cairo or London. All American citizens, most of them Greek Americans, were allowed to abandon Greece.

The Greek army in our western mountains, until recently so gloriously successful, was dispersed without official orders, in confusion and anger, while politicians in Athens were making the decision to collaborate with the enemy. A few courageous generals and their brave soldiers met the German war machine at the Metaxas Line, on the northern border to Yugoslavia and further east toward Bulgaria, while our exhausted fighters on the western front were left leaderless to drift angry and discouraged back home.

> I am now four years old and this day finds me sitting on the stoop in the neighbor's yard. My head is bent. I am brooding, following the path of an insect in the dirt. My friend Dinos taps me on the shoulder. "Katinítsa, Katinítsa, your daddy's back!" I look at his big eyes, his high upper lip protruding, and I don't believe him, because he always looks like he's smiling. "Shame on you, fooling me . . ." I respond, my hope wild but controlled,

a dry sob in my throat. I don't want to be crushed. Better not to believe than to be disappointed.

"Honest to God, I saw him."

"You are not allowed to swear," I retort, already didactic. His eyes are eager; my lips begin to tremble. "Dino, if you are lying, I'll have my brother beat you up."

"No, you got to believe me. I saw him going in your house."

I stand up, paralyzed for a minute, and then I run home. There is much noise in the entrance, the door left open, and my mother's glowing face, the other children jumping with joy and confusion. A stranger comes toward me, but he wears dirty rags, his face unshaven, his arms open. No, no, this is not my daddy! "Katinoúla," he says, "Katinoúla." But I burst into tears and hide behind my mother's skirt. The film of that day ends there.

He soon threw the rags away and my mother burned them in the yard. Bathed, in civilian clothes and clean-shaven, he became my beloved Babás once again. The uncles had also returned to their homes and our families found their centers again. At night we gathered around our father. He started telling us stories of the war on the mountains while our world went to pieces all around us. The barbarians were already at the gate.

There was something about his stories that reduced me to tears and sobs. I don't remember his telling, but I remember my hurt. I didn't want to know of his terrible days and nights on those frozen mountains. In the telling I was there with him and the pain was unbearable. "I don't want to hear any more, Babá. Stop." And here is my brother's voice taunting me: "You're such a baby. Go away. We want to listen to him." And my father's hand caressing my face. "It's her imagination. She can see what I'm describing. Don't make fun of her." Was it good or bad, this thing inside me? The overwhelming sense of feeling what he felt? Life would give me the answer.

On 10 May 1941, something remarkable happened in Athens to re-mind all Greeks that courage still burned its constant flame among the occupied. I am not certain how word reached the rest of Greece since the news was suppressed, but the Greeks were used to underground communication through many ages. Two young men, Manolis Glezos and Apostolos Santas, climbed the Acropolis rock, not through the Propylaea, the ancient entranceway to the sacred rock, but along the harsh rock surface. They then lowered the hated swastika and raised the Greek flag. It was a momentary act of defiance, but its light burnt for a long, long time.

The sadness of missing husband and father shows on the mother's and children's faces. February 1941.

Katohí (Occupation)

... because the barbarians are coming today.

—C. P. Cavafy, *Waiting for the Barbarians*

One more memory of the year I was four remains etched in my brain as seen from that same apartment window that was opening the world to me. Our street led from the square of the Makedonian Ministry building, the beautiful edifice that separated Old Thessaloniki or Ano Polis on the hills from the new one built after the fire of 1917. From our street to the waterfront most of the buildings were newly built but without character, stacks of apartments with their individual balconies. Very few of the old, gracious structures remained. Since Thessaloniki was situated as in an amphitheater, the streets had a downhill incline and led first to the old Roman *agora*, which at that time gaped as a huge dug-out hole, and then, through the elegant Aristotelous Square, to the sea.

The Aegean Sea

9 April, 1941. I am leaning out of that window, searching for the familiar faces of little friends while my mother's fingers keep a firm hold on my dress, lest I fall. It's a quiet morning, and for some strange reason, no one walks in the street. A distant roar begins, something like thunder; it makes my tiny body tingle though the day is sunny. My mother now rises and stands behind me. I sense fear in her, in the street itself. The roar becomes an approaching crescendo. French doors to the balconies open, but the people do not emerge. They stare from within, without expression. No one applauds as a green-gray stream of motorcycles turns the corner and rushes downhill. I see them still, those drivers, their eyes hidden under helmets, on those cycles with the side cars, leaning their bodies in unison as the street curves and this hostile river of German uniforms turns and passes by. The faceless enemy has arrived and the barbarians have entered the city.

Soon afterwards we moved to another street and another apartment, higher up, with balconies in the front and back of the building and with much more light. The street, named for a general, was one of several that radiated from the Makedonian Ministry square and had not yet been paved. Carriages passed occasionally, pulled by horses, but they were soon replaced by one or two scraggly mules, since the Germans requisitioned all transport animals. Running water rarely streamed from the kitchen and bathroom faucets because the enemy utilized most of it. Together with my two older siblings I learned to walk to the communal cistern up the street, toward the small Langadá Square, and there we three waited to fill our clay water pots. Even

I had a small one and tried courageously not to spill any of the precious liquid as side by side we tramped gingerly back home and up two flights of stairs. Electricity became even more scarce and then nonexistent. At night we sat around the table, an oil lamp, its glass chimney washed and the wick trimmed carefully every day, hanging from one of the walls, another one on the table. We told stories and learned to read by that limited light. I remember that the shadows were long and mysterious on the walls. Shadows that moved and became eloquent as Daddy talked. My baby sister, just starting to talk, marveled at how large her hands appeared on the wall. I missed those shadows when electricity returned.

We played in the street. There was no car traffic to fear. We knew what to avoid. Barbed wire had sprung everywhere like thorns on the body of wounded Hellás, the land we loved. We were children, and children play even in streets that hide danger, when there are no yards available. The electric substation at the edge of our block was a reminder of exploding bombs. One day, as was our habit, my friend Poula and I had drawn the familiar outlines of a hopscotch pattern on the dirt and were hopping on one leg from square to square when two German officers passed by. They paused and watched us and said something one to the other. *Should I run home?* I stopped hopping and, my eyes lowered, I stared at their fancy leather boots. Finally they moved on at a leisurely pace as though they were taking a pleasant walk. We stared at their backs, but we had lost interest in the game. I ran upstairs. When I described them to my mother, she said, "Maybe they were remembering their own little girls at home."

I was dumbfounded. "You mean, these men have children?" I couldn't believe it. They were the enemy. People with children were human, like my parents. These men were something other, something alien.

In mid-century, Thessaloniki was a fairly large city with the character of a village. Walking everywhere within the city limits as we did, we came to recognize faces and personalities. We knew whose smile to return and whom to avoid. Even we children knew the names, direction, and importance of the main streets and businesses; the famous sweetshops, especially Flokas, was familiar to everyone, as were the few grand hotels and restaurants. We, members of the Katsarka clan, walked to the narrow Païkou Street, to that third-story hall we called "our church," almost every day of the week. On Sunday mornings, walking downhill along Ionos Dragoumi Street, we passed by every door and building as familiar as those of our own neighborhood. Close to Egnatia Street there was a large restaurant, Elisia, with its adjoining hotel, both now occupied by the Germans. They were the lords of the universe. We could only stare open-mouthed at their wealth and the lavish meals they ate sitting around their white-clothed tables. Their women wore their blonde hair upswept and even they appeared powerful in their uniforms. My father and mother looked straight ahead, but holding on to my father's hand I craned my neck to see them, those strange creatures who wore new uniforms, who looked clean, as though they were using up all the soap that had disappeared from our homes, who spoke with loud confidence to one another while we whispered about them. We resented them while envying them. I hated the sounds of their language.

Hunger and Cold

Around me gather all the little faces of Plaka . . .
skeletons, all eyes. Eyes full of bewilderment, eyes that do
not understand. What is there to understand? That the
earth is dried up?

—Ioanna Tsatsos, *The Sword's Fierce Edge*

Winter 1941–1942. In one of the great ironies of history, the first winter of the vicious occupation was the coldest in memory. Sunny Greece was turned into dark, icy gloom, as if all the gods had decided to have macabre fun by conspiring against her. We could have endured the cold had we had enough to eat. In Athens people were dying in the streets from malnutrition and starvation. They dropped where they stood and were picked up like so many sacks of useless matter, thrown onto open carts to be taken to common graves. The occupiers grabbed precious foodstuffs and commodities for their troops and their own cities, making it obvious that as long as they, the superior Aryans, had enough for life, the rest, specifically the Greeks, could go to hell. It didn't help that the Allies had blockaded the seas so that no supplies could arrive inside Greece. In depriving the Germans, they left us without wheat and other necessities for living. Who would have the courage to protest? We were deprived of our humanity, and the starving have no energy for protestations.

Our father, a wise and careful man, had bought, early on, cases full of raisins, walnuts, chestnuts, and almonds. The apartment had no extra storage space, but he hung a curtain in the bathroom behind which he stored supplies for the lean months that arrived all too soon. The words "black market" entered our daily vocabulary. I could not imagine a marketplace that was black, ours having been so colorful, but I soon learned that this black abstraction was both good and bad. Though my father disapproved of black marketeers, he was forced to buy from them in order for his children to survive. Thessaloniki, close to the fertile plain of Makedonía, did not suffer the terrible fate of Athens. Farmers, furious that they had to relinquish all their produce to the enemy, reserved enough to sell to their fellow Greeks. Thus we did survive. But many—the very poor, the recent refugees and their children—did not.

It was our parents who worried about food. We children knew almost nothing of their agonies. Occasionally, they offered us tiny glasses of beer to make the dishes seem more palatable, since it was so difficult to make food tasty without our beloved olive oil, lemons, and good bread. Reports from Athens that people were dropping dead in the streets from starvation were frightening as well as obscene. In a culture where the dead are honored, remembered, and called *makárioi*, "the blessed ones," the fatalities were not reported to the authorities so that the living would not lose their precious ration cards. In Thessaloniki, a city with thousands of middle-class Jews, it was mostly the very poor among them, the ones who performed the most menial of jobs, who now, left without any income, were dying of hunger. The rest of the citizens, whether they liked it or not, were forced to deal with the black marketeers and independent, stubborn peasants in order for their families to survive.

There was no oil for heating. Where my father found the occasional coal or kindling, I don't know. There was a wood stove in the living room, and the first sign of the morning, was the smell of the fire as Dad lit it, followed by the homey aroma of crumbs burning as he toasted the bread on a grill on top of that stove. But again, this may be a later memory.

Of all Daddy's continuous efforts to keep us fed and alive, one instance comes to mind, together with its accompanying tremors. The offer of the whole pig must have come from a farmer who knew my father, but we never learned his name.

It is a summer day that holds a secret, but we don't learn it until later, in the night. As curfew approaches, our mother becomes frantic and tells us that Babás has gone to a neighboring village to buy a pig. Now night is falling fast and there is no sight of him. The street is eerie in its quiet. This is another one of the weird effects of occupation. The Greeks—night people who in good times leave home in the twilight to walk to the *tavernas,* to the theater, to restaurants, singing when alone in the street or conversing in loud voices that carry to the open windows when in company—these Greeks are now forced to stay inside. The shutters and French doors to the balcony are open, and we sit inside, in the dark, waiting to hear some sound that would signal our father's arrival. It is past curfew time. We are all dressed for bed, but our mother stays in our bedroom instead of hers, and her worry pulsates in the room, reaching each one of us, making us very quiet. The youngest is asleep. Trying to get me to sleep also, my mother lies down next to me, but I am so restless that she reprimands me, "Can't you just be still for a few minutes?" How strange that her irritation at me looms very large in that long, scary night. I try not to move, but when, for what seems the hundredth time, she goes to the balcony, I follow, together with the two older children. It is dark everywhere, but there is enough light from the blessed Greek sky that seems always filled with stars and the light of the moon to see the street. The picture in my mind now is of an open cart down below, a pig, obviously dead, lying in white splendor on it, there, under the balconies. My mother's relief, like a new atmosphere, engulfs us and reaches even down to my father, who looks up at us and motions us to be quiet. "He is home, he is home," we breathe, and all of us run downstairs quietly to offer help.

I have no recollection of how the pig was brought upstairs. What happened to the cart afterwards? Was there another man with my dad? These are questions that I am asking when it is too late for answers. I will never know. I do remember that Pappous, our grandfather, was in our kitchen on the following days making sausages. How they accomplished all that in a small apartment kitchen is beyond memory and even my capacity to imagine. Apparently, that pig, which almost cost Daddy's life, fed many members of our extended family. I bless its memory.

A.D. 1936

Memory is the scribe of the soul.

—Aristotle (attributed)

As I am writing these vignettes, I wonder: Is it possible for us to remember the events of the world while in our mother's womb? What if they stamped us with their angst or joy? How much is memory, how much is feeling, how much depends on distilled stories? Besides nourishment, what else entered us through the amniotic fluid?

I spent nine months of the year 1936 in my mother's womb. I was to hear the names and the words that she reacted to during those months repeated to me again and again in the coming years until I believed that I had heard them while she was carrying me. Here is my crucial list.

Falling under the category of *ominous*—*the first sign:* The Spanish Civil War, the first realization that war is coming for all of us.

The second sign: Haile Selassie of Abyssinia. A king, a black man, flees his country because Mussolini invades it, his airplanes pouring death with chemical weapons upon the poor Ethiopians. Mussolini makes it clear that he does not consider them human beings.

The third sign: On 4 August Ioannis Metaxas declares himself Greece's dictator. He is not a bad man but he admires the Nazis and is merciless to Communists. From that time on, 4 August has a distinct connotation for all of us. *Augustianá* we call this time of loss of freedom. Democracy, in the land of its birth, is abolished. Communism becomes the great enemy, the word to fear. Intellectuals and ordinary workers, together with the old democrats, the Venizelist officers of the army, are sent to exile, to deserted Greek islands. (Eleftherios Venizelos's name had already become a code-word for those opposed to both fascism and the monarchy.)

The fourth sign: Franco becomes the supreme leader of Spain after a bloody civil war, as another Fascist, like Mussolini and Hitler, consolidates power. Bad men are winning during this year.

And, falling under the category of *hopeful*:

Jesse Owens offers the first worldwide recognition that light-colored skin is not the only biological reality worth admiring. Jesse, his black skin glistening like dark burnished metal, wins four gold Olympic medals in Berlin under the nose of Hitler, who has proclaimed that only white Aryans matter in the world.

Is there a category for *indifferent*? On my birth day, a silly man, King Edward the VIII, abdicates the English throne because he loves an empty-hearted American woman. He too admires the Nazis.

And so I emerged into the world somehow knowing a great deal. For instance, Haile Selassie and Mussolini were names familiar to me from the time I could hear. That latter name would echo again and again in the years of my childhood as the harbinger of evil, the incarnation of Satan—Mussolini. I had to learn the story behind everything I heard. The Greek humor and poetic bent created satire, limericks, and songs about all these events. My mother, however, could not face any event with a light heart. She loved her husband and her children with a passion that would become her downfall. She met all the news with the agonizing question: What does this mean for my children?

My father would record later that the first seven months of my life were joyful for the family. But then, on 3 August 1937, the first blow fell and nothing for us would be that carefree and joyful again. In late July, my mother showed signs of illness—loss of appetite and a persistent cough. The first doctor to see her ordered *ventouzes*, the cupping practiced for centuries from China to Greece. The cups were made of glass with their edges turned upward so that they were smooth where they touched the skin. Daddy would dip a small torch in alcohol, light it, place it briefly inside the cup to heat it, and then he would apply the warm cup on the back of the patient. It made a funny sucking sound when removed, leaving her back like a surface of large pink circles. Afterward, he would rub the whole surface with alcohol and cover it with a woolen cloth, so the warmth would permeate and last. Mother's illness persisted and worsened.

Three decades later, my father wrote down in painful detail the events of 3 August, 1937. A famous doctor, Haritanis by name, arrived at our house at four in the afternoon. He listened carefully to my mother's back, paying special attention to the upper right side. In his no-nonsense manner he announced: "This is where the trouble is. She must stop nursing the infant immediately. All her eating utensils must be separated from those of the rest of the family. She is contagious. You must take her for an X-ray tomorrow and for lab analysis of the sputum. She has tuberculosis." I was in my crib; the two older children, wide-eyed, clung to our father, while our mother, sitting hopeless on her bed, wept her silent, huge tears. My father, dumbfounded, listened to the cold medical voice that pronounced the end of joy for his family.

Father's ordeal had just started. Members of the various Katsarka families who feared the dangers of tuberculosis divorced themselves from our own tragic unit. My grandparents, as they were to do again and again in our lives, stepped in to take care of me, the infant, while the aunt who lived in their house took my sister and brother in her care. The tuberculosis diagnosis was confirmed by the X-ray, and the doctor ordered the patient to be separated from us and to move to a nearby village recognized for its clean air for those suffering from the disease. At that time, the diagnosis of TB was as frightening as that of incurable cancer in our days. Few were the ones who survived.

Our mother, maybe because she had been abandoned by her parents as a child, was not able to stay alone. Without her children and her husband near her, she was dying inside. Her depression was profound. She was only twenty-five years old. For that reason my long-suffering grandparents took me with them to live in the same house with my mother, in a nearby village. My father hired a good housekeeper to care for the home and my mother, and then he split himself in three, as he put it, to care for all of us—his business, his two older children at his brother's house, and us four in the village. Public transportation consisted of overcrowded rickety buses. Twice a day he bought fresh food and groceries and sent the packages to the village through the bus company. My grandfather climbed up and down the hill to pick them up and bring them to the house. And little by little, her youth, the rest, good food, and constant care made the difference for my mother.

The village and the sanatorium were built on hills four thousand feet above sea level, though the location was only twelve kilometers from the city. The French had first populated the area of Asvestohóri when they found its atmosphere beneficial for their sick soldiers during WWI.

The very few photos of those days show me with my grandparents, my parents, and the housekeeper. I have a huge forehead, no hair, and I am eager to walk. I am not smiling, but my gaze is quizzical. My mother is not holding me.

When winter arrived and the X-ray showed that the lung had healed, we returned to the city. We stayed in our grandfather's home, on the second story, until all danger of contamination had passed. The only tale told to me about those months was that of my near death. I suspect it is exaggerated. Many of the homes of the day preserved a remnant of Ottoman heating—a brazier made of copper, a large elaborate disk sitting atop an attractive tripod base. The disk hid a bowl in which charcoal burned until it was white hot, then the cover was removed and this contraption heated the room. We were all taught, early on, that we should crack a window for fresh air to come in, to avoid the danger of carbon monoxide. One day, the housekeeper was holding me on her lap, warming herself near the brazier. Both she and I fell asleep. When my grandmother entered the room, she was horrified at my bluish color and rushed me to the balcony, thus saving my life. And there the story ends.

When we returned to our own apartment, Daddy said that we resumed a happy life. But the year was 1938 and clouds were gathering all over Europe. What they rained on all of us was not blessed water but fire and death.

For me, the difference was that now I could speak and words filled my head and protected me from many fears.

Between the months of my mother's first illness and the war, we lived in an apartment at a corner of Kassandrou Street. The exterior was yellow stucco and our balcony was on the third story. From there I would call out to the neighbors who sat in their own balconies, and I became a kind of mascot for them. A child's first words are always precious, but mine apparently never stopped. The neighbor women would invite me to their apartments, and I would entertain them with my stories. They probably plied me with sweets. Across from our balcony was a small jail with a large courtyard. The guards roaming the yard must have been very bored. They called up to me, "Katinítsa, Katinítsa, tell us a story." The road was narrow, there were no gardens and no cars, so the street itself served as the neighborhood yard. We knew everyone by sight, if not by name, so it was not strange that a little tyke of two would carry on conversations with the guards of the low-security prison. I made them laugh and that was all that mattered. But it was also the beginning of the craft of making up stories. Stories would save my life. This is the only memory I have of the time of peace—*stin irini*.

Words were precious to my young ears. I listened hungrily even when I was not paying attention. During that wondrous and fearful time of early awareness, between 1940 and 1945, I kept hearing the longing in the voices of the adults around me. In my family there was very little silence when grown-ups gathered. The stories they told held within them a phrase that made something inside me tremble. "*Stin irini*," they said again and again talking of the days before the war. They didn't say, "before the war," before the cursed Germans arrived; they said, "*Stin irini*." It meant: "in the time of peace." *What was that?* and, *When was that?* I wanted exact answers. For I knew it was more than just a date, and in the telling of the stories I sensed that the time of peace was way before 28 October 1940. Peace had lasted up to the early months I spent in my mother's womb.

The adults talked of the horrid Hitler, who seemed to dominate so many of their conversations, and of an ineffectual Brit named Chamberlain. Hitler hadn't sprung out of nowhere just before the invasion, as my young mind had imagined the monster's arising. He had been around a long time before, and no one had done anything to stop him. *Stin irini*, people could travel from city to city and from country to country. Imagine traveling to another country! Words and names filled my ears and stored themselves in my mind:

Churchill, London and the BBC, Mussolini, Goebbels, Bucharest and Belgrade, Budapest, those mysterious B's that spoke of old civilizations and intrigue, and then the freezing Leningrad, Russia, and Stalin. They swirled in my mind, some with that special fascination of foreignness and others with the dark of terror in them. All I had to do was listen to the change in tone when the names were uttered, and then I knew what to feel. "Fascists," they pronounced with disdain, "Nazis..." and the words made all of us tremble. We didn't know their meaning, but we knew their horror.

Names: Mussolini made grown-ups spit. *Hitler* brought nothing but darkness. And then there were the brand new words: *curfew.* "What is a curfew, Babá?" "Nobody can be in the streets during curfew. We all have to be at home." Gone were the nights of Greeks returning home in the dark, singing on the way, always singing and laughing; or the sound of a lone man's steps returning home, whistling, to keep himself from loneliness in the night. *Sysitio* was another new word—soup kitchens. Why do people have to go there? Because they have nothing to eat at home; they are starving. *Lice.* Is that why all the boys have shaved heads?

The litany of dreaded words continued: *barbed wire.* "Don't go near it, my children." Sometimes, behind the wire, we saw thin, pale, terrified faces. "Halt, Raus!" were the barks that made us jump. *Concentration camps.* I remember the cold of the words as they invert their order in the Greek, the misery they brought to the imagination of a child who did not know at that time that other children were imprisoned there. And yet, something inside me knew.

Stin irini, it had been different. I used to stare at a snapshot taken before my birth. My father and his brothers were sitting at an outdoor café, heads thrown back, laughing. Imagine sitting in the open and laughing as if nothing evil lurked in the shadows, for there seemed to be no shadows in the photo except those created by light. What was it like to live *stin irini*? These days we lived *stin katohi*, in occupation. The reality of my childhood: Occupation. "Babá, why are we the slaves of these people? What have we done?"

Nothing. Greece wanted to remain neutral, but Mussolini, the buffoon, dragged us into the war for his own personal arrogance. He wanted to show Hitler that he too could invade a country and win. After Hitler moved into Rumania and her rich oil fields, Mussolini went berserk. He thought Greece would be a walk-through. He started all kinds of provocations, like the sinking of the Greek cruiser *Elli* on one of the holiest holidays for Orthodox Greeks, on 15 August, the day of the Virgin. Metaxas ignored all provocations so that Greece would not be drawn into a war. But the narcissist in Italy persisted. And look at what happened. We beat the pants off the ridiculous Duce, but still it cost us our freedom. We have forgotten how to laugh, we have forgotten how to sleep without worry. The years of occupation pass very slowly. Will we ever live *stin irini* again?

We Are in God's Hands

*I have said this to you, so that in me you may have
peace. In the world you face persecution. But take
courage; I have conquered the world.*

—John 16:33

From the earliest awareness of self, I knew I was not alone. I am sitting on my Daddy's knees, facing him. Still the youngest in the family, I have the attention of both parents. Years later, my father will say, "It's impossible that you remember anything from that apartment. You were not yet three!" But I do remember.

We are on the balcony. It's night. The moon full, its light kind, lets me see my Daddy's face clearly. Mammá is sitting next to him. They are both smiling, they are both relaxed—such a rare memory of peace. I touch his face and then I ask, "Babá, if I find a long, long ladder and climb up, up, up, can I touch the face of God?" My parents look at each other and their eyes ask: Who *is* this child? And then they hug and kiss me.

The longing for the Divine has been within me from the beginning. That much I know. And in my family, this longing, nurtured daily, became a passion. We prayed together every night to a God who seemed close by and real to my parents. So, for us, God was as real as our Daddy. How soon after our births did he start reading the biblical stories to us? I don't know the date, but I can vouch that not a single night passed without the stories of weird men and women with ancient names imprinting themselves on our brains. Noah and the dove and the preposterous march of the animals into the ark. Joseph and his mean brothers were as present to me as my daddy and his own brothers. How I wept over that story of abandonment. But life was not meaningless, our father taught us. Someone is always with us, guiding us. "We are in God's hands, my children," he would tell us later, when the bombers flew overhead. So, the little girl, the child, knew from the beginning that God cared for her.

We had the measles in that apartment, my brother and I at the same time, and I see the doctor coming to examine us. Tied to that memory is a sewing needle that slipped from mother's fingers and her frantic warning to us: "Don't walk barefoot. The needle can travel through your body. Be careful." Why do I remember that needle and that warning?

Daddy's voice is always there, telling us stories and giving us the assurance that God loves us. They had such certainty, those men in the Katsarka clan. It started with their father, my beloved Pappous, the one who had the courage and the gall to defy the powerful Orthodox state church, to break away, to start his own house church centered on Bible reading and on certainty. None of his five sons defied him. We gathered to read, sing, and pray. And we were always together, either in the hall we called *ekklesia* or at grandfather's house. Our extended family was filled with joy and laughter, together with the assurance that God loves us, that we belong to God, that we are in God's hands.

I went to bed seeing it and feeling it. There was an image that kept me safe. God's enormous palm holding us lovingly, never letting go, cradling us, keeping us from harm. Nearly ten years would pass before I allowed the first doubt to come knocking, before I felt the curve of that hand loosening and there I was, falling, falling.

The moment I was old enough to know that our family was somehow different from other Greek families I started asking questions. How did we come to be different from our fellow Greeks? I want to know, again and again. Why don't we go to their beautiful churches, why don't we make the sign of the cross, why are we *different*?

> We are five families, bound together by blood, united under a strong grandfather and a mild grandmother, so we can easily consider the rest of the world unnecessary to our happiness. Since we also worship together with unfailing regularity, the illusion that we are sufficient unto ourselves seeps through and offers a dubious emotional security. We are the Katsarka clan, but what gives us this permission to be different?

Pappous

The story is familiar but I never tire of hearing it. The beginning of this separation from the world started in our grandfather's teens. It's a story that for some of us, as we grew older, became a myth of pride; for others, their own sin of pride made it a cause for shame. After all, they said, he was only a cobbler.

Grandfather, our *Pappous*, was given the name of one of the church fathers, Athanasius, one of the strongest defenders of the Holy Trinity, but from what little is known of my great-grandfather, no theological ambition or knowledge accompanied the naming of his only son. Yet, our Athanasius (known as *Thanasis*) grew up to become one of the staunch defenders of the faith, having the courage to speak against the established church, thus becoming, like his ancient namesake, "Athanasius *contra mundum*"—"against the world." Being left an orphan after his mother's early death, he was not particularly loved by his father and stepmother and was forced to work as a tailor's assistant under harsh conditions. In his birthplace, Adrianople, in that bare shop, he was often trembling with cold and hunger, but so obviously intelligent that he, a poor Greek child, attracted the attention of an educated Bulgarian. (The ambition of the Bulgarian authorities at that time was to turn Greeks into Bulgarians, my father would explain to us later, because they wanted to lay claim to both Thrace and Makedonía, two important Greek provinces in the north and northeast of Greece.) So, young Athanasius was sent to a Bulgarian school, where he learned their classical written language much better than his own written Greek. When he reached his seventeenth year, a Protestant missionary gave him a New Testament to study, and that was the transforming point of his young life.

He approached the local Orthodox priest: "Father, why is it that we are not worshipping according to the way of the first Christians?" he dared to ask; to express criticism of the Church to its eastern wing, a church that acknowledges no mistakes and no need for reformation, was a huge mistake. He was quickly booted out. A small Protestant community already existed in Adrianople, a result of those upright and courageous New England missionaries of the nineteenth century who dared to evangelize in hostile territories, foremost among them the Ottoman Empire. Soon he found a home among them, much to the displeasure of his stepmother, who observed ritual Orthodoxy to the point of fanaticism. (This last word was my father's whenever he talked of her; later I came to realize that my father often used *fanaticism* for those who disagreed with him theologically.) The passion young Athanasius felt for his New Testament faith was all-consuming, so when the time came for him to choose a wife, he listened to his missionary friend, who advised him against agreeing to marry one chosen by his parents. "I have the perfect girl for you," the missionary told him, "a girl who deserves her name." Málama Petrides lived in Constantinople with her mother and two brothers. The popular modern Greek word for gold is *málama,* and the girl was indeed good as gold. This arranged marriage would last for more than sixty years of love, faithfulness, sadness, and utter devotion. My grandmother was always present to us in her long black dress, her black shoes, her wavy black hair lightly tinged with gray, pulled into a bun. I don't ever remember her dressed in color. I remember her sad smiles, but never her laughter.

When Athanasius was forced to leave Adrianople right before the start of the First World War, he gathered all the members of his extended family with him and they arrived in the fatherland as Greek refugees. There he started the house church that would eventually become the Free Evangelical Church of Thessaloniki. Those of us who were born into it and those who came to our family by marriage were enveloped in its teachings and culture, and in a sense we too grew to be *contra mundum*: we rejected an established state church, which to us seemed a substitute for nationalism, and we avoided its theologically indifferent adherents. They didn't make an effort to know us and we didn't make an effort to notice much beyond the externals that were interwoven with the culture.

We attended church regularly and faithfully. The members of our congregation did not smoke and the women wore no makeup and dressed modestly. The men were faithful to their wives and they didn't step into *tavernas*, clubs, cinemas, or any other places considered worldly; above all, they didn't gamble. Ballroom dancing was forbidden to men and women. The men went to their shops or offices, did the midday shopping, and returned home; the women took care of the house and of the children. Sunday mornings and evenings were spent at church, and every weeknight, except for Mondays and Saturdays, was also filled with church activities. This was our world, and since we knew no other, it was for us the best world. It must be admitted that all these evidences of morality and clean living gave us a feeling of self-righteousness and superiority.

We children were taught not to participate in activities that our congregation disapproved of; we studied and determined to excel in our studies so that the Katsarka name and the church's name would be honored.

Yet to be a cultural Greek was to be a Greek Orthodox— whether one was a believer or not—so inevitably we Protestants were politically suspect to the various successive gangs that took over the government of the country. But like the Orthodox, we thought we were in the right, and everyone else was wrong. "Orthodoxy" means "correct dogma or worship," something that seemed ironic to us, who of course worshipped exactly as the early Christians had! We really believed this. This conviction made it easy for us to carry the burden of being different.

YIAYIÁ MÁLAMA

When I think of my childhood, my greatest regret focuses on my grandmother, on my failure to ask her questions about herself. I learned most of her life events from my father, who adored her.

She hailed from Constantinople. It's impossible for non-Greeks to understand the depth of feeling associated with the name of that city now known as Istanbul. For the Hellenes of early twentieth century it was still *the Polis—the* City—as though there were no other city to compare with it. It had been the seat of Byzantium for one thousand years, and Byzantium to the Greeks was equated with Greek Orthodoxy; therefore, it was Greek! The language of Byzantium had been Greek, and so the Greeks claimed it as their own, even after its fall to the Ottomans in 1453. The Greek population that, through the centuries, survived and endured within the Ottoman Empire was for the most part educated, wealthy, and proud of their heritage until the forced exchange of populations in the 1920s and the Greeks' expulsion from Constantinople in the 1950s.

Women who hailed from Constantinople were excellent cooks, and my own Yiayiá deserved this cliché without apologies. Sweet Málama's life was so filled with tragedy that I couldn't stop to think of it when I was a child. I had to grow up, to become a mother and grandmother in order to understand the depth of her sadness. Her father died when she was a child, leaving a wife, a daughter, and two sons, orphaned. One of the sons left for America as a young teen, never to be heard of again. The second son, a handsome youth with black eyes and curly hair, survived only to die a horrible death. Chased by the so-called Young Turks in their greatest madness at a time when they were killing Armenians in the streets, he never recovered. He looked like an Armenian, so when they chased him, holding their curved knives in their hands, he barely escaped; he reached home, shut the door, and was never the same person again. The doctors decided that the extreme terror had made him mad, and he was in and out of the horrid insane asylums of Adrianople until he died, still too young and in despair.

My kind, loving Yiayiá bore six sons and one daughter whose name was Katerina. I was the only one of the granddaughters named after her. Katerina died of a heart condition at age twelve. Yiayiá's baby boy also died of scarlet fever when he was only an infant. One day, when my own father was still a child in Adrianople, he was walking with his father and one of his father's friends by the river. The child Vassilis heard the voice of his own father filled with unbearable grief as he said

Thanasis and Malama Katsarka with their five adult sons.
My father is second from the left.

quietly to his friend: "This is where we buried him." That tragic voice stayed in my dad's memory. In the last year of his own life he said to me: "I thank God I have not outlived any of my children."

These were the grandparents who time and again left their own home, their own room, to stay with us when war and tragedy hit us with the illness and death of our mother.

Images and Sounds of War

> Then, sad, I went out on to the balcony
> Went out to change my thoughts at least by seeing
> Something of this city I love,
> A little movement in the street and the shops.
>
> —C. P. Cavafy, *In the Evening*

I remember the bleak days of occupation as gray. That is the predominant shade that colors my memories. A gray pall had fallen on the city. Every street seemed to have an entrance that was blocked by barbed wire. Huge gray stones covered openings that led to the basements of buildings. Men, women, and children walked about in the same clothes—coats, pants, dresses, and skirts—that were mended and patched again and again. If a sweater wore out, the women of the family would unravel the wool. I can still see their calloused hands rolling it expertly in a ball; blended with the wool of another worn sweater, it would be knitted again into a different cardigan. "Just like new," they would say, shaking their heads. Nothing was thrown away.

My father checked our shoes for holes and then, putting them on a last made of iron and expertly shaped as a foot, he would cut an outer layer of hard sole leather to fit it. Next, using a sharp knife especially made for this leather, he would shape it, afterward sanding the edges. Placing it on the bottom of the shoe, he would hammer tiny nails all around the surface and there it was, ready to be worn another season. Except that children's feet had a tendency to grow as the seasons came and went.

The boys went about with hair shorn down to the skull. We were all terrified of *psires*, the lice that plagued people without soap. Boys wore short pants even in winter, their socks droopy and loose above their shoes, their legs and bony knees always chapped and red from the cold. Chapped hands and knees were not only an annoyance but a constant pain.

The cleverness of the Greeks was apparent in their inventiveness. A seamstress would come to the house for a whole day or two. Without patterns, she would remake old clothes with attractively placed ribbons, buttons, and strips of cloth so that they looked new, or at least different. Having a sewing machine in our home was a huge luxury. I looked with utter fascination at the foot of the seamstress pressing the pedal rapidly, pushing the cloth with expert fingers. Her skill of looking at a photo and copying it into a dress impressed me enormously.

Every now and then there was enough money for new dress material. I remember exactly where Mother's favorite shops were in the city, for we walked there with her. I loved entering those fabric stores. They were lined with shelves that held dozens of bolts of silk or cotton. The smell of colorful cloth wrapped around those flat rectangular boards was so clean and inviting that I felt as if I had just had a bath. The best show was put on by the seller, who was always a man. Mother would point to one of the bolts, he would take it down, and then, in a fluid motion, he would whip his wrist unraveling the cloth, which undulated on the counter like a wave of sea water. I smelled again that fresh clean smell and dreamed of it as a dress fashioned on my mother. And then the salesman would joke about my mother's exceptional ability in bargaining, something everyone practiced at a time when prices were fluid. Everything else needed

for dressmaking we bought from a tiny shop in a corner of Venizelou Street under the famous and unfinished Caravan Sarai. There
was room inside for only one person, but every needle and bobbin,
every color thread imaginable was stacked in excellent order inside
that miniature shop, and the proprietor knew where to find it. I remember those years of extreme specialization with much fondness.
Acquisitions and corporate madness have never appealed to me. Even
as a child I was filled with admiration for those who made a living by
selling tiny things in a most personal manner.

The sounds of the streets entered through the open windows, but
inside the home we loved singing. Mother sang when she cooked or
did housework. She had a lovely soprano voice and had married into
a clan of gifted singers. The neighbors called her a nightingale. The
melody of *La Paloma* brings her to mind with a poignancy that still
hurts. Every night we sang our favorite hymns, prayers to God for
peace. Outside our home, the nights of the war years were mostly
silent. No one sang in the streets. Even the birds seemed to have
fallen silent. Every now and then a harsh voice would echo to reach our
balconies with dread: *Halt!* "Someone is caught after curfew. Some
unlucky person is ordered to come out of hiding." These became familiar sounds hated as bitterly as were those who uttered them. Among
us we whispered the other words that were synonymous with death:
the SS, the Gestapo, the terror of concentration camps. I remember
the icy feeling that ran down my spine when I heard them. We shiv-
ered both with cold and with fear. That's the memory of occupation
that never leaves. And the howl of the sirens, the howl of sirens.

Quotidian — And Life Goes On

Thessaloniki. Our beloved city,
mother of refugees, mother of the poor. Here we have
lived as children.

— Zesiades, *Thessaloniki, then . . .*

The reality of wartime is that people who are occupied still have to get up in the morning and face the day. Fathers wear their one remaining suit to work, no matter how worn the sleeves and patched the elbows, and a fedora on the head. Mothers get their children ready for school and spend hours struggling with the excruciating task of finding something to cook so the family can eat and survive. Survival is what matters. Daily life continues.

There was a conviction that the Nazis were determined to exterminate the Greek race, no matter their early protestation that they had arrived as people who honored our ancient glories more than any other of the European nations did. Instead, Goebbels made it clear that he did not care about the Greeks dying as long as his army was fed. Wheat and olive oil disappeared. Our raisins, olives, and meat were destined for the occupiers and their families back home. So everything of value left the country while nothing could enter Greece because the Allied navy had blockaded the seas in order to keep materiel from reaching the enemy. And so the Greeks starved.

After months of this criminal indifference by both enemies and allies, the Brits were persuaded by the International Red Cross and by Greeks living overseas to allow Swedish ships to bring in the first relief supplies. From August 1942 on, the supplies increased and the terrible famine, *limós*, ended. Hunger, however, would persist for years.

That year of the famine I started school. An educational institution with a serious reputation, my school was named for the city where it was founded—Alexandroupolis—east of Thessaloniki, where the hated Bulgarians now practiced their reign of terror, allowing only Bulgarian to be taught in the schools. So, the excellent faculty from Alexandroupolis came to Thessaloniki, and we were the fortunate ones, chosen to be taught by them. In those first years my primary school was housed in a crumbling building up on the hilly Old City. I remember it as being near the Monastery of Vlatadon, which dates from the fourteenth century. (My cousin tells me it was on Kassandrou Street, but I cling to the image in my brain.) I climbed over the dirt mounds and the rocks of unpaved streets, struggling to get to my class on time. The first day, when scrubbed, eager, and alert, I sat at my desk, I faced my first public disappointment. I was so proud that I had already learned to read. I announced it to the teacher, but her response knocked the air out of me. "You are going to learn the alphabet as *I* teach it; whatever you know, you have learned wrong." She was an ugly spinster with a large nose and thick glasses. Her voice sounded nasal, something I had not heard before, and I developed an instant dislike of her.

One of my girl cousins was in my class that year. She was pampered, and we suspected that her father bribed the teacher with food. The only thing I am sure of is that my mother was angry because Toula was favored by this teacher. I learned for the first time that my mother thought my intelligence vastly superior to my cousin's when, to my surprise, she arrived at the school one day. It was the only time

*My third grade picture with the teacher I didn't like. My cousin
stands next to teacher's left and I am next to my cousin.*

anyone in my family interfered with my schooling. My mother argued
with the school authorities over their favoritism, but I was profoundly
embarrassed. She never interfered from that day on.

※ ※ ※

Did my brother walk with me up that difficult hill? I don't
remember. If he did, he probably moved far ahead so he would not be
seen next to me. Did they let me walk to school all by myself at such
a young age? I think they did because they had no other choice. My
memory is of walking alone. I don't remember an adult ever walking me to any of my schools, and school buses did not exist. As the
months passed and I adjusted to the routine of the first grade, I was
asked to read aloud to the rest of the class. "Let Katerina read it," the
kids pleaded and even the teacher agreed. Words started tasting good
in my mouth and their sound delighted my ears. A love affair began,
one that would never end. Reading books and reading aloud: Was
there a greater pleasure?

The view from that hill known as Moni Vlatadon was stunning, but little children rarely pay attention to views. Yet, it remains imprinted in my brain even though my cousin tells me that's not where the school was located. From our kitchen balcony we could see the monastery and that connection again was one of familiarity and beauty before the ugliness of television antennae on top of apartment buildings ruined it.

When I was in the fourth grade, the whole school moved to the center of the city, near Ayia Sophia, the beautiful Byzantine church that dominates its square. Again, it was a long walk from home, and in the winter it was painful. We had no thick socks, no boots, and certainly girls never wore anything but short dresses. Even the boys suffered in their short pants, no matter the weather.

Despite the occupation, though, the sun continued to rise and set and life's routines, though painfully curtailed, continued.

During daylight hours, the streets in front of the apartment buildings were filled with sounds. Everyone who sold or fixed something sang out his wares and his craft. There was a little dark-skinned man who repaired the tin of much-used casseroles, together with various pots and pans. He smelled of metal, and his skin seemed to have a sheen on it that also looked and smelled metallic. He was one of the many Roma who lived in and near Thessaloniki. I can still see the silver bubble at the end of a pointed tool that he dipped into hot molten metal. With a sizzling sound, he attached the bubble to the holes on the bottom of casseroles. The silver cooled quickly and the pan could be used again. All our pots and pans looked patched. Nothing was thrown away.

Another man walked the streets carrying a long bow with a taut string. Whenever he was called from one of the balconies, he climbed the stairs to the top, taking over the terrace of the apartment building where ordinarily we hung the wash. His work could only be done on a day when the terrace was free of sheets, towels, and pillowcases. He carried the mattresses upstairs, undid their stitches, pulled out the cotton filling, and then, like a musician, he plucked the string of the enormous bow through the cotton to stir it and fluff it. A rhythmic sound accompanied his labors, a vibration similar to the strings a low bass makes, a nonstop humming as he worked. After he refilled the mattress cover, he sewed the seams back together and the mattress looked twice as fat as before. Everything had to last through the war years. There was no way to replace anything.

A third itinerant worker whose song drifts back to my ears sang his ability to sharpen the knives and the scissors of the housewives. These men, Gypsies we called them, carried all the needed equipment on their backs and walked from neighborhood to neighborhood day after day. I marveled even then that there were so many different jobs—so many difficult, painful jobs—that people created and performed in order to survive, so that their children could live.

A few farmers who became familiar through the years would come to our door to sell fresh vegetables from their gardens in the countryside, together with precious eggs. And Daddy knew where to go to find us fresh fruit. When he did, he carried it home in a netting made of white string. We were the lucky ones.

Our milkman was a favorite of ours. He arrived with his mule laden with long, capped, tin containers—slender cylinders filled with fresh milk. He carried one of these upstairs, always cheerful, whistling; we were already at the door because we recognized his whistled songs. We held our own pan carefully underneath the spout as he poured the milk, sometimes still warm from the cow, into it. We paid him the few drachmas; I am sure they were not enough to compensate for all that labor. He was faithful and he never missed a morning. In better times, his mule led his cart, but during the war even the mules were taken by the heartless conquerors and he had to push the cart himself. Together with the milk he brought news of the countryside to our father. So we knew that the villagers suffered much more than we did, as they had done through the many centuries of Greek life. What lay in their future would be much, much worse.

Our neighborhood, like most in the good days, was self-sufficient. On the same block there was a small shop that carried, in small quantities, all the immediate needs of a household, a small version of a general store. Cumin, used in all ground beef dishes, and cinnamon could be bought there in tiny, white packages, thin papers folded expertly like envelopes around the spice. There was a separate hole-in-the-wall that carried fresh produce. Since a Greek cook cannot do without fresh parsley or dill, these were available green and dewy at that little *manáviko*. At the other street corner was the butcher, who could cut exactly what we needed on the spot, while another shop offered the ever-present yogurt in small, round, red ceramic pots. Our street smelled delicious because a small factory made the famous *biscotta*—small sugar cookies. (Borrowed from the Italian, the ending in Greek changed from "i" to "a" to form the plural of *biscotto*.) And the baker who cooked our meals in his vast beehive oven also produced fresh loaves of bread for us every day. All that went by the wayside, though, when supermarkets arrived.

Our favorite snacks centered on nuts, dried fruits, and roasted legumes. We passed by tiny storefronts that sold *revithia*—chickpeas, salty and roasted. For a drachma the vendor would roll a piece of paper into a cone, fill it with *revithia,* and hand it to us, still hot from the charcoal. Roasted almonds, mixed with raisins, were delicious too. Before Coca-Cola and its ever-present, oppressive advertising, there was *gazoza*, a fizzy, lemony drink so welcome in

*Doritsa, Kostakis, Katinitsa, and little Niki—a formal
picture taken before our mother's death.*

the summer. Electric refrigeration was unknown, so the iceman was our friend. He hooked a block of ice from his cart, wrapped it in a piece of burlap, and then it took two of us as we struggled to climb the stairs carrying its wet weight.

And so, day after day, the lucky ones survived.

Ekklesia and Prayers

Greece, of and for the Christian Greeks.

—Georgios Papadopoulos, leader of the 1967–1974
junta when no freedom of religion was allowed

To be a Greek is to be a Greek Orthodox. So everyone told us. We Katsarka children learned early that this designation had more to do with national identity than with religion. Nobody really bothered to ask us what we believed. No one cared. But they did care that we were different; therefore, not wholly Greek. There was one religion teacher who was fascinated by the Katsarka children who seemed to be in every classroom in the primary school. He looked at us with amusement and cared enough to ask us questions. The first half of the fifteen Katsarka grandchildren did exceptionally well at school. When the younger ones succeeded us, this same teacher said to my closest boy cousin: "The Katsarka dynasty is crumbling." We thought it hilarious. The rest of the teachers ignored us or tried to make us feel inferior. But for us, in our budding and lively evangelical community, our faith was also our identity. We didn't doubt that we were Christian, but we never doubted that we were also Greeks.

Our lives revolved around the family and the *ekklesia*, a small rented hall that served as our church. Free Evangelicals, we called ourselves, but the Orthodox hierarchy, the state church, considered us heretics. Ecumenism was then unknown. Our *ekklesia's* leadership— chiefly, my grandfather, his oldest son, Constantine, and my own father—refused to align themselves with any European or American denomination. They were sure that their movement was indigenous, started by my grandfather in his home after he and the family arrived from Adrianople to Thessaloniki. Above all, they considered themselves free.

There were only two days of the week when that little *ekklesia* was not open—Monday and Saturday. The rest of the week, it was our second home.

On Sunday mornings, Mother dressed us in our one good outfit. She had washed and ironed every item of our clothing. The most prominent for the girls was a wide length of taffeta starched stiff so it would stay in a huge bow on top of our hair, the one distinctive fashion statement of those poor years. The bow was larger than our faces and it stayed in place if we didn't run. On my baby-fine hair, though, it slipped and hung on my cheek instead, and I was glad when I outgrew it. Our youngest was little enough to be carried in Dad's arms, but we three older children held hands and followed our mother down familiar streets. We were surrounded by the names of poets in Thessaloniki. Ionnos Dragoumi Street led to the Via Egnatia, famous because of the Romans, famous because of St. Paul. We crossed its tram rails, and within a block, we turned right into the narrow alley that housed the business buildings, that smelled so different from our residential street. There was something metallic in the air.

The pavement was cobbled as we entered Païkou Street, very narrow, very familiar, with the door of Number 4 open on the left, and then that chasm of the uncovered basement that was always dark below the stairs. I didn't dare look into that darkness. We ran up the two flights as quickly as we could to enter two more doors and then the beloved room we called *ekklesia*. There was no central heating. A wood-burning stove was lit and stocked by one of our poorer members who had found a home in that room and went early to make it as warm as possible before the service started. There were no pews. The individual chairs were cane-bottomed, arranged in rows, with one central aisle: one wing for the men and one for the women and children.

Our hymnbooks were hardback and small enough to fit in a pocket or a purse. They contained no musical notes, just the words of the hymns. Gifted congregants from Athens had translated English and German hymns in rhyme, but in the archaic, artificial Greek language called *katharevousa*, the "pure" language. What everyone spoke (except for my father, it seemed to us) was the *demotic* language, the one used in daily life, from the root *demos*, "the people." We sang with gusto. I don't think there was anyone in that room who could not carry a tune, and in the desperation of those days they all sang their love, their passion, and their longing to a God who was very real to them. "Oh, Jesus' my song will be your name . . ." and, "What a friend we have in Jesus, all our griefs and sins to bear. . . ." The griefs were many. The shoe soles had holes in them, the clothes had been mended many times, the overcoats barely covered the body (much less the legs), and food was so limited that everyone was thin and pale. But "Return to take us, Lord Jesus," they prayed, and the desire for a heaven was very real, palpable, in the present misery they longed to escape.

It's winter, 1943. The pervasive grayness of the occupation smothers the city's breath but it does nothing to alleviate the cold. Thessaloniki is open to the wind known as Vardaris from the Vardar River of Yugoslavia. Vardaris rushes toward the sea, alongside the river whose name now becomes Greek—the Axios River— blowing tiny dust tornadoes on its way. The sandy soil hits us and burns the skin. Our legs are always bare;

knee socks and long stockings are unknown. We are holding hands while walking with our parents to our church. It's Wednesday evening. Already dark. The air smells of burning wood in stoves.

Prayer meeting night. Church for us is not one of the beautiful Byzantine buildings that adorn the city. For us it is simply *ekklesia*, the calling-out of the people to gather in one place, as in the first century, in the time of St. Paul. In our familiar hall on Païkou Street, we gather as if at home. There is a large platform with a lectern against one wall facing rows of chairs—the left wing for the men, the right for the women. We children always sit up front, on the side of the women's wing.

One of the uncles is preaching tonight. We sing a hymn and then everyone kneels on the wooden floor, our faces toward the seat of the chair, our elbows on the woven cane. I lean my forehead on my arms and listen. The voices are those of men; why is no woman praying aloud? Even though I don't pay much attention, I recognize the voices and I know what they will pray for. *Kyrie, Kyrie,* they cry. *Come soon, come and deliver us.* I need no explanation for this plea for the Second Coming. Life is hard. Food is scarce, dangers lurk everywhere, but within these walls there is the conviction that God truly cares for us and we will not be abandoned. No one seems to realize how selfish we are to think that God belongs just to us. I hear them offering every woe to this very personal God.

Some of the men have wives who refuse to attend this "heretic group of infidels," and these men are the ones who pray most fervently. Later, as we walk home in the dark, I overhear Daddy laughing with one of his brothers. "Iordanis was praying with tears again tonight. His wife must be nagging more than usual." They chuckle quietly, but kindly. They are the fortunate Katsarkas with their devoted wives and healthy children. Our walk home becomes a little lighter.

Other walks I remember are also filled with theological themes. Returning one night from Grandfather's home, I am holding my father's hand, as always. He is talking to one of his brothers. They are discussing the crucifixion. My shoes touch the cobblestones which, subconsciously, I count, but my hearing is acute, focused on the words the men are speaking. They are talking of Jesus' suffering on the cross. And I, young as I am, think: "It is terrible that Jesus was crucified. But if he *knew* that he would be resurrected, it could not have been as terrible."

I didn't know it then, but this was at the heart of what would become my search for the Jesus of Nazareth who transformed our world. Grateful as I am for my upbringing in the faith, I acknowledge how much my community lacked in their understanding of the human Jesus, of *kénosis*, as we pronounce this word that means "emptying," and of the Incarnation.

During those difficult times someone donated a pump organ to the *ekklesia* and my older sister and I took turns playing the hymns while the congregation sang. We found such comfort in the place we called our church. I remember with affection the men and women who greeted me with a caress on the cheek, a smile, and the very Greek,

"Ach, Katinítsa, Katinítsa," a kind of sigh with the affectionate version of my name that revealed—what? Fatalism, love, a future wish? I could never figure it out, but I accepted the kindness of the greeting.

Several of the regulars come to mind. There was a very thin poor man with thick glasses who served as sexton. He looked cold every time I saw him. He would arrive early to light the stove that provided the only heat in the winter, making sure to arrange the chairs in neat rows. I also remember Mr. Foukas, with his white hair and long mustache, a beautiful old man who adored my mother and who, after her death, turned all his affection to me. In his youth he had been one of the handsome Greeks chosen as *evzones,* the ones who stand as guards at the Tomb of the Unknown Soldier. He cried more than my own grandfather did when I left Greece at sixteen. Our little congregation was welcoming to the poor and strangers, especially during those terrible war years when everyone was poor. But, like most evangelical churches, it was also exclusive: only the approved redeemed could partake of Holy Communion.

For us children most of the service was a bore until we started a choir around our family piano, and then everything changed. But that is another story.

The Piano

There is geometry in the humming of the strings;
there is music in the spacing of the spheres.

—Pythagoras (attributed)

One of the bitter regrets caused by my mother's early death is not knowing what our lives would have been like had she lived, what immeasurable love she would have poured on her grandchildren, and, above all, what would have been her own accomplishments had she had the chance to study. She must have possessed a high intelligence because, with limited literacy, she gained a more than superficial learning of the subjects that interested her. She had a beautiful singing voice, causing some to call her a nightingale. She was very quick in everything she did—her unrivaled housekeeping skills, her cooking, her interest in her children's minds, bodies, and demeanor. My mother knew all the neighbors by name, showing affection for some and disdain for others. She had a ready reserve of nicknames and a caustic tongue, but for several she showed admiration and respect.

The apartment building adjacent to ours housed a family with two older girls. Their balcony was one level lower than ours, so we could see them quite well when they sat in the evenings to chat quietly, as we also did with great regularity. My mother liked their mother, though the two women, as was the custom, called each other by their last names, never omitting the prefix *Kyria*—Mrs. The girls' names were rather unusual—Zana and Pepy—and they were serious university students.

We looked up to them, especially since in addition to their erudition they played the piano. What was it about the piano that so attracted my mother, who had never attended a concert? She determined that her three girls would learn to play that glorious instrument. She must have discussed her passionate desire with the neighbor, who referred her to a family who needed to sell their own piano. Sadly, the daughter of that family was dying with tuberculosis. Our father was not inclined to spend money on things that were not absolutely essential to our survival, but our mother knew how to persist when she was in the right. She didn't ask for much. She was used to hardships and even to poverty. But she was adamant when it came to her children's welfare, so she insisted that my father buy us that piano.

The piano arrived while I was at school, hoisted outside the building to enter through the balcony, I was told. It was a full-size upright, black, with candle holders, which were immediately removed because my mother didn't like them. The piano tuner pronounced it in excellent condition with a magnificent tone.

Lessons began immediately. The teacher, a Greek who had emigrated from Russia, arrived twice a week in her worn black hat and Astrakhan coat with its unique curly fur, recounting the glories of her past life. My mother tolerated her and, sensing that the woman was suffering in genteel poverty, fed her with the afternoon tea. We girls found her easy to fool and uninspiring. But we learned the notes within a week and understood the time value of each note—whole, half, quarter, eighth, sixteenth. We learned not only to recognize them but to create our own musical staff, drawing the five lines and then filling in the notes as directed. To this day I hear melodies with *do-re-mi-fa-sol-la-si-do* in my mind, and I sing notations whenever I hear music. I fell in love with the sound of the Italian words: *allegro* and *andante, arpeggio, appoggiatura* and *adagio*. From this teacher I first heard the word *samovar.* Did she bring one to the house to sell to us? I have a vague image of one, but then it disappeared.

She was soon succeeded by another teacher, an accomplished pianist, who stayed with us to the end. I was a quick learner with sight-reading ability, but I didn't have the passion that would cause me to practice for hours. I enjoyed showing off. Very soon we were playing hymns. The hymnody of our church community was very different from the Byzantine music played with relentless regularity over the radio. Ours came directly from our Western fellow Protestants. The intellectuals in the evangelical community translated the rhymes into purist Greek and for years we sang the tunes without any musical accompaniment. I suspect that this was the primary reason my father gave in to the purchase of the piano; he wanted his daughters to accompany the congregation. I don't remember who gave the pump organ to the church, but we learned to love it.

The piano in our home became a great attraction to cousins and friends. We spent hours playing and singing in groups. In those gatherings we discovered that the Katsarka clan could sing beautifully. Every one of us—those born into the family and those who came to us through marriage—had a lovely voice, an unearned gift that we cherished. So we took singing for granted. By the time we became teens, we had, among the cousins, a perfect balance of soprano, alto, tenor, and basso voices. After we found the score of a hymn, we would spend hours together writing down the notes for each voice. We delighted in the harmonies and practiced with verve for hours on end. Our grandfather thought it pretentious, but the rest of the congregation started delighting in the sounds of the choir. Eventually, as with most Protestant churches, it became a kind of performance instead of being integrated into the liturgy, but that took from us none of its profound enjoyment.

Dangers of the Day, Terrors of the Night

Honor to those who by the life they lead
define and guard a Thermopylae

—C. P. Cavafy, *Thermopylae*

Later we would say how lucky we were that we, the whole clan, survived the years of occupation. But we did not know then that waking up each day to face the unknown, the unpredictable, was an agony for our parents, so much so that my father would later call the occupiers "those anthropomorphic monsters." His first encounter with the superior Aryans was immediately after the invasion. My father, at a time when all footwear was handmade, sold leather—uppers, insoles, and soles—for shoes and boots, and all the small nails and tools used in the making of them. Two Nazi soldiers entered his store together with one of their Greek stooges. One of the soldiers, seeing the shop's trap door open, descended to the basement and emerged carrying an armful of rolled leather. He then looked at the shelves and motioned for more products to be placed on the counter. The total, in the dictated economy of the day, came to fifteen thousand drachmas. When he saw the bill, the German started yelling, threw one-fifth of the cost on the counter, grabbed his loot, paused, turned to my father, placed one hand on his gun holster and then exited, followed by his two comrades. The myth of central European civilization that my father had so admired crumbled.

More dangerous was the morning when a group of young soldiers on bicycles passed by Dad's door asking for directions. The one in charge held a map of the city, and Daddy, not knowing German, started explaining the route in English—a huge mistake. All those Hitler youths, filled with hatred of the British by their leader, reached for their pistols. Daddy kept his cool and switched to Greek. The representatives of the superior race cursed him and continued on their way.

Much, much more dangerous was the time Dad was accused of dealing in the black market. The sad reality of occupation wherever it occurs is that it gives the opportunity to those who disregard morals, who love money more than honor, to become traitors to their own people. Some came from the slums of Thessaloniki and others from that particular, odious class of war profiteers who would enrich themselves during the terrible years to emerge as the nouveau riche after liberation. The details of that adventure are difficult to follow even now, even after my father wrote in exhaustive detail what happened in terms of his business. What I remember is the fear, the worry, and the tears.

Our mother had to take us with her wherever she went. Too young to be left alone, we accompanied her because she had no one else to watch us. So what I remember is the two older ones holding hands, my mother with the baby cradled in one arm, her other hand holding on to me. We walked city block after city block, all the while knowing that our mother was frantic and weeping. But we heard and remembered the ominous words: Pavlos Melas.

This was initially the name of a hero of the struggle for the liberation of Makedonía from the Turks. Unfortunately, his heroic name was given to a section of northern Thessaloniki at the city walls, one that at that time housed a concentration camp. So it became infamous, ringing like a death knell whenever it was uttered during the war years. Imprisonment there meant death. Whenever the Germans were bent on mass retaliation, the officer in charge of the execution squad would deliver an order to this prison. He would enter, and without any particular reason, he would call out names of random prisoners who then would be taken out and shot to death. Our grocer had sold one liter of olive oil at an inflated price, had been betrayed, and had been shot as a result. My parents knew of that gruesome result. On one terrible day in 1941, one hundred and one prisoners were taken behind Pavlos Melas and executed. Eyewitnesses reported that they marched to their death singing, "Goodbye, sad world."

The fear that our daddy would be taken to that hell hole was enormous because someone had accused him of selling leather at a higher price than allowed. For three days, while he was being held in police custody, our mother and we four would go from one official to another begging for his life. We started with our own uncle Harilaos, who had been assigned as dentist of the police force, so his word carried some weight. His advice and the lawyer's good sense kept my father from saying anything self-incriminating at a time when he was filled with confusion and fear. My mother, despite her despair and constant weeping, managed to go to everyone who might help her husband. I remember our last visit to a judge, though I had no idea what the crime my dad was accused of happened to be. Later I was to learn that it had to do with which part of the cow the leather in question had originated! The laws of occupation were so unpredictable that it was extremely easy for the enemy's stooges to accuse honorable citizens of crimes. A hefty bribe to the accuser changed the terminology of the supposed crime (the location of the leather on the cow) and the judge, who happened to be renting from our mother's aunt, set our daddy free. How easily death could arrive those days and how thin the line between life and death was.

Our father's worst adventure, however, was yet to come. The most notorious of the collaborators in Thessaloniki was a man named Papanaoum.

In the years between the wars he was unemployed and lived on handouts. He had found his way to our evangelical congregation and attended a few times, probably expecting financial assistance, and then he disappeared again. When Greece fell to the enemy, he found his niche as the most traitorous of collaborators. He even had an office in the Germans' high command building. My father, inadvertently, had been instrumental in the imprisonment of Papanaoum's chief lackey.

This is how it happened. The street where my father had his shop was named Valaoritou, after one of our great poets. It was filled with small businesses of every kind one could imagine, and the storekeepers knew one another. Many of them were my father's friends. Several came to warn him that something bad was about to happen to him, and it did. He was summoned to Papanaoum's office. As soon as Dad entered, the traitor grabbed my father by his lapels and shook him: "You, Katsarka, how dare you accuse my friend? Don't you know that I can have you shot? You think you are a Christian, don't you? Well, look here, look who really is a Christian." To his horror my father then saw this criminal open a closet filled with little children's shoes and with pretty outfits for girls and boys. He knew immediately to whom these had belonged. His horror increased as the thief continued his harangue: "I have cleaned Thessaloniki from the Jewish filth. Whenever I see one of them I send him to Cracow. That's what it means to be a Christian." My father, nauseated, could not speak while Papanaoum now screamed his orders. "You will go to the state prosecutor and retract the statement that put Antonis in prison. If you love your children, you will do as I say, or else you will end up in the same prison as Antonis. Choose!" And with that, he pushed my father out of the door.

With his ears burning from the voice of the man who considered himself omnipotent in the climate of occupation, Daddy walked the length of Paralia, the waterfront way, to the justice building. It just so happened that there was a conference in process, but they let him in. The judges turned in surprise while my dad found the courage to tell them exactly what had transpired in Papanaoum's office. "He threatened my children's lives," he concluded, "but I am a Christian and will not lie to save myself." Then one of the judges of the Court of Appeals stood up and said, "Thank you, Mr. Katsarka, for your testimony and your courage. We were just now discussing this same situation. I can tell you this: The Germans are pitiless and hardened tyrants. But in matters of justice, not once have they overturned our decisions. We will look into this matter. If anyone troubles you, I, Efenis Galanós, will come to rescue you."

My father left, returned to Valaoritou Street, shuttered his shop, and came home to consult with our mother. That night, two of his friends from the business community knocked on our door to find out what had happened to him. The whole city knew of Papanaoum's cruelty and vengeance and everyone feared him. My father told them that he was firm in his decision not to lie to save one of the traitor's lackeys, but they said: "We love you, Vassili. We don't want to see you destroyed. Papanaoum can easily send some of his scum to place Communist propaganda inside your shop and then have you arrested. He has done it to many innocent citizens." My parents lived with this fear for several days and sleepless nights, but the threat never materialized. My father, as was his constant habit, attributed his rescue to God's mercy. Within a year, this same Papanaoum, taking with him all that he had stolen from Thessaloniki's Jewish population, followed his Nazi gods as they departed Greece in disgrace. Word reached Thessaloniki that the train carrying the evil man was bombed. But the reality is that, even after liberation, many of these collaborators were never punished.

Another Winter: The Jewish Tragedy

> I refuse to accept the view that mankind
> is so tragically bound to the starless midnight
> of racism and war that the bright daybreak
> of peace and brotherhood can never become a reality . . .
>
> —Martin Luther King Jr.,
> Nobel Peace Prize acceptance speech

In the recurring dream I am standing on the balcony and the body of the girl upstairs floats horizontally before my eyes on its slow descent to the ground. She's wearing white. I remember nothing else. No noise, no blood, no contact with the ground—just that white-clad body falling in front of me, as I am standing there, unable to stop it.

(Years later when I ask my father and older sister about the girl upstairs, they look at me the way they used to when I was very little and came home to tell them of my imaginary adventures outside. "*Fantasía*," they would say, half smiling, half worried. "She has such *fantasía!*" They repeat it now. "No," they say, "there was no girl who fell to her death."

"I remember she was Jewish," I insist, and they raise their chins in the characteristic Greek negation.

"It didn't happen. The things you imagine . . ."

I leave it at that because I know that the next memory that haunts me is very real indeed.)

It's a terribly gloomy day, cold and rainy. I am standing at the closed front window looking down at the street, sadder than a child of seven ought to be. I am looking at a girl who seems to be waiting on the sidewalk across from us. She is older than I am by a few years and she is wearing a dark green sweater. On the sleeve of her sweater the star of David is sewn, badly patched on in yellow, but I can see it clearly from the third story. I pull my father's sleeve. "Babá, what is that?" And why is it making me so sad, I think, so sad that I am weeping?

"She is a Jewish child," Daddy explains in a dull voice. "The Germans have ordered all the Greek Jews to wear that sign on their clothes. It's called the Star of David." I know the stories of David; he is one of my dad's biblical heroes. Nothing makes sense. That must have been the first night I dreamt of my neighbor upstairs falling, falling before my eyes.

I have very few vivid memories of my mother's healthy years. One of them is of the day she was confronted by the immense tragedy of our Jewish neighbors. A long, ancient, and famous street crosses the central section of our city, from west to east. It is the Via Egnatia, the one St. Paul followed as he moved from Philippi toward Thessaloniki. One of those great Roman roads that made it possible for the empire to conquer the world of their time, it reached as far west as the Adriatic and as far east as Byzantium. Every time our mother went shopping she would cross Egnatia Street, walk through the short Kolombo arcade to come out on the other side and to our father's store. We all liked the arcade because that's where our parents first saw each other and fell in love without ever exchanging a word. Both Mammá and we children crossed it often.

> On this sunny day, I remember her return home. She is terribly pale and out of breath and leans heavily against the sink where she has placed the squid she will eventually wash, and I, fascinated but scared, will watch the black ink run out of the strange fish. But now my mother can't move. She says to my grandmother, "There were thousands of them passing on Egnatia Street and I couldn't cross for a long while. Thousands upon thousands walking toward the railroad station. And the harsh German soldiers guarding them, pushing them. Where are they taking them?" Her large green eyes are cloudy. We must have asked questions but I don't remember them. What I do remember and I wish I didn't is what she says next. "There was a little old woman standing next to me and she said aloud, 'It serves them right. They killed our Christouli.'" And my mother— who married into a Protestant family and espoused faith passionately—is she appalled by the statement of this ignorant woman who thinks she is defending Christianity?

I continue to examine this phrase through the years. To avoid understanding the Christian faith and its demands upon us, we make our religion easy and trivial, keeping Jesus a tiny child in a manger and calling him by a diminutive name, Christouli, a name that does not allow him to grow into the prophet whose truth and justice scared the religious and political authorities, a truth thoroughly ignored to this day, especially by those who claim him as their own. And for so many Greeks, who would much rather pray to his mother, he never seems to grow into the Christ. He remains the little baby, Christoulis. In America, the fundamentalists have made him into an idol in their own image, one who has no relation to the Jesus of the gospels.

The Jews of Thessaloniki had dominated the culture and the economy of the city for a very long time. As the war was beginning, there were more than sixty thousand Jews living in Thessaloniki. The terrible exodus that my mother observed that day was the beginning of the end for the majority of them. We as children did not comprehend what was happening, but the gloom of that day when I first saw the Star of David on a girl's clothing and the tears and bewilderment of my mother remain with me like the dream of the child falling before my eyes. And there I was, unable to do anything to help.

We had lived together without distinctions or separations for decades—Greeks, Jews, Armenians, even Turks. Thessaloniki was multicultural and harmonious, except for the Gypsies, who dressed differently and were mostly poor—we knew many of them only as beggars, and our culture was not kind to them. But the Jews were like us. Their stores were numerous and we shopped there without thinking, *This is Jewish.* The nicest merchants on my father's business street were Jewish, and we showed them the same respect we showed to the Greeks. So it came as a great shock when the toy store next to my father's place no longer existed. Daddy tried to soften the blow by telling us that the owner, who had always been so kind to us, had moved away, but something in his voice was not right. I heard him asking my mother what he should do when Jewish friends begged him to keep some of their treasures until their return. I do remember that Mother agreed with difficulty that he could purchase only a short fur coat because the woman selling it needed the money immediately and desperately.

There was a prevailing sadness in the city, a disbelief that something so evil was happening to our friends and fellow citizens. The horrific words, concentration camps, were heard, but no one was prepared for what we learned about them after the war ended. And we children were kept in the dark about the whole tragedy—except that we dreamed dreams of death and falling.

Requisitions

> Greed makes man blind and foolish,
> And makes him an easy prey for death.
>
> — Rumi

All the beautiful buildings of the city designed after the great fire of 1917 were now brimming with German uniforms. The hotels were full of the occupiers and their families, who found life in Greece much more luxurious than that in wartime Germany; for them, Greece was a sunny heaven. They were mad about our sea and our food—olive oil and raisins, bread and cheeses—and the country's unrivaled light. Without shame, they ate and reveled while Greeks died. The only Greeks who approved of them were the collaborators. I knew instinctively that this was a dirty word.

Soon another one was added to the frightful words of occupation: *requisitions.* Collaborators with the enemy belonged to the lowest stratum of humanity and even the suspicion that one worked with Germans would cause us children to cross the street to avoid him. Soon we were also to learn the meaning of requisition, when on a Friday morning two men arrived at our apartment. One of them, Topouzelis, said he was now the owner of the apartment; the other one held a paper signed by a German: "Requisitioned by order of Herr Wentzel." Our original landlord was angry because rents were frozen during the war and he thought my father rich by comparison to himself, so selling the apartment to a collaborator was his revenge. The new owner,

Topouzelis, a known collaborator, marched in, ordered one of the bedrooms emptied, locked its door, pocketed the key, and demanded the key to the outer door. He told us that his wife would move in on Monday. We had no choice. We, the powerless, stood speechless before the orders of the powerful.

In an apartment with only two bedrooms, a small dining room and a living room, one bathroom and one kitchen, we six would be forced to share with people we did not know and did not like. It was unthinkable. Our father, when he came home, was stunned. He went to the local Greek authorities, who told him they were powerless because the order had been signed by a German official. Saturday came and, silently, we watched our mother's unending tears and my dad's face drawn with worry, as he prayed silently and aloud, "O, God, have mercy."

That afternoon we heard a knock on the door and a familiar voice calling our mother's name. "It's Aunt Ida!" we cried and opened the door. Flushed from rapid walking, smiling her kind smile, in came Ida, who was not really an aunt but was so beloved that we couldn't call her anything else. She was originally from Crete, where an English aristocrat had met her family before the war. Ida's father was widowed with a number of children, unable to care for all of them. The Englishman offered to take Ida to his home in England. She had spent a few happy years with the British couple, but when war broke out she returned to Thessaloniki to keep house for her two bachelor brothers. This was the fate of many unmarried women in Greece. She was my mother's best friend, and the only one who continued visiting us later, even after the onset of the disease. We four loved her.

When she entered that afternoon, she saw immediately that something was wrong, so Dad explained the danger of losing our privacy and our home. Ida tried to comfort Mammá and then she left to visit the sick as she did on Saturdays, promising to return to us later. There was a makeshift hospital on Venizelou Street, just a few blocks away, where the sick and wounded were housed in crowded medical wards affording them no privacy. One of the men from our church was hospitalized there and Ida, giving him the news of the community, told him of our predicament. The patient on the next bed heard our father's name and interrupted her. "Sorry, Miss, but is this *Vassilis* Katsarkas you are talking about?" When Ida agreed that indeed it was, the man sat up. "Tell me what the problem is," he asked her, and she did. Then came the surprise: "Go back and tell Mr. Katsarkas to speak to his friend, Dimitri Economou, who is now Dangalos's first officer. He will help him. Go back and tell him, Miss."

Dumbfounded, Ida returned to us and shared with my father the man's suggestion, word for word. Ida said, "Vassili, I know this is God's hand in your life, but who is this Dimitris?" Daddy shook his head and a long, strange story emerged. But first, a digression.

Soon after the occupation, many soldiers who had fought in the war against Mussolini took to the formidable Greek mountains to escape the Nazis and Italians and to create a resistance movement. This grew to tremendous numbers and by 1943 was seen as such a threat to the occupiers that Hitler sent many more troops than he had intended to fight against the resistance. But the Germans didn't know how to fight in our mountains, so they emptied the prisons of thieves and even serious criminals to train them into a rightwing movement that did their bidding against fellow Greeks. These were the notorious Security Battalions, dreaded and despised even by non-political, law-abiding citizens. As collaborators they wielded power in the cities, and everyone feared them. At the same time all of Greece was gripped by another fear—that after liberation we would fall into the hands of the Communists because German propaganda, Greek nationalism, and British paranoia insisted that all the resistance movement was Stalinist.

Near Thessaloniki, a sheep merchant by the name of Dángalos had seen the Communist guerrillas massacre his own brothers, and from then on he was bent on revenge. He moved to the city and created a strong army of his own Security Battalion, spreading fear throughout Thessaloniki. Dad described him as tall and handsome, one of those heroic Greek types made even more impressive because he dressed as an army officer. His headquarters were in a hotel at the end of Valaorítou Street, where Dad's business was located. The revenge tactics of Dángalos and his followers were scary because they were so unpredictable. They would enter businesses and homes to drag men away just because someone had accused them of being Communists. Word of mouth would spread every morning about the corpses found in outlying neighborhoods of Thessaloniki. Terror gripped the city.

So we could imagine our father's worry when on a certain day, one of these battalion members arrived at his shop with a large shopping order. After Dad fulfilled the order, the man said, "Package everything and follow me. You will be paid at headquarters." With trepidation Dad followed him but was shocked when he was indeed paid in full. As he was exiting their office, he was met in the corridor by Dimitri Economou, a classmate he had not seen since 1916, dressed now in a sergeant's uniform of the Security Battalions. They hugged as Greek men do and then, as my dad was leaving, Dimitris said: "Vassili, if anyone bothers you, you come to me; do not hesitate." *God forbid*, Daddy thought to himself, *that I would ever turn to a Security Battalion traitor.*

And now, months later, Daddy found himself rushing to the hotel headquarters of Dángalos. It was getting dark and Dimitris was preparing to start his nightly patrol. He paused long enough to listen to my father's story, and then he said: "Vassili, go home and sleep peacefully. First thing Monday morning I will speak to this Topouzeli. Don't worry."

On Monday morning we were all trembling at the thought that the new owner would arrive with his wife. My father went to find Dimitri, who said, laughing: "Don't worry. I spoke to him and he was so scared, he wet his pants. He will do nothing against you." So it was that our home was saved.

After the war, the landlord apologized to my father and said that Topouzelis was very frightened that Dad would betray him as collaborator. My dad didn't even bother to answer.

Four Winters

> These are the winters of our discontent
> Made inglorious by the sons of Hun
>
> —paraphrasing Shakespeare, *Richard III*

Most of the war memories take place in winter.

Winter 1940–41, when Daddy was at the front. Loneliness, fear, running to the bomb shelter, and the first bite of *bobóta*—a nasty-tasting and foul-smelling bread made with rough cornmeal ordinarily reserved for animal feed. No olive oil. But I was a very young child and little else remains in memory.

Winter 1941–42—the terrible months of the famine. That first winter of the occupation was the harshest of them all. It was impossible to know what was going on outside Greece. Travel had become a memory. A few ramshackle buses remained, but there was no gasoline for trips outside the city. The tram on Egnatia Street still ran its course, every inch of it inside and out crowded with tired human beings; there were so many clinging to the outside of the tram I kept wondering what was holding them up. People still went to work. Shops opened, however meager the produce on their shelves. Businessmen and shoppers carried money in large string bags since inflation lost all bounds and a loaf of bread, if found, cost a million drachmas.

We were isolated and forgotten. Yet, somehow, word got out that the Greeks were dying. The Germans were rapacious and the

Allies had blockaded Greece so that nothing could enter by sea or land. Now, the small country that had given so much of value to the Western world was in danger of extinction. There were still people on the outside who remembered "the glory that was Greece" and who cared.

Where the radio came from I don't know. The brothers buried it in Grandmother's yard and when we gathered there on Sunday nights, it was brought to a room where, with the doors and shutters closed, the five Katsarka brothers would bend over it to hear the thrilling words: "This is the BBC." Daddy would translate in whispers. So we learned that the International Red Cross was demanding entrance into our sad and abandoned land. Eventually, that gloomy winter of 1941–42, the year of horrors, led to the spring and by late summer the famine came to an end and people stopped dying in the streets. But the hunger continued.

Winter 1942–43. Slowly, painfully, the Germans who had appeared invincible started losing. But 1943 made them even more frantic to carry out the most barbarous exterminations in order to please their evil, maniacal leader. And the Italians who had lorded it over us—especially over the Athenians—were so happy to be rid of Mussolini and to abandon the Axis alliance that they danced in the streets and hugged and kissed the Greeks.

Winter 1943–44. Waiting for the end, waiting for liberation. Greeks were expecting the Allies to land on our beaches but they delayed, preferring Normandy and Sicily. Thousands of leaflets dropped from airplanes and we rushed with laughter to pick them up, to read them before the Germans caught us. Young boys defied danger by posting them on building walls and by writing graffiti proclaiming the desire for Allied arrival. The Nazis, mad with supposed fears of a Communist takeover, enlisted disaffected Greeks to join the Security Battalions. The end would be very bad for us.

For a very long time I thought it was the Nazis who came to bomb us at night. It was with a shock that I learned later that the planes belonged to our own allies.

At first, after Daddy left for the Albanian front, it was the Italians who flew overhead to perform their haphazard bombing of Thessaloniki. Most of the time they arrived in daylight, something that made both the bombs and the running to the shelter less ominous than the night raids.

Years later, in remembering his days on the front, Daddy would marvel that the Italians were not more devious, more clever in their timing and targeting; how easily, he said, they could have eliminated whole battalions on the mountains. Fortunately for the Greeks, the Italian air force missed opportunities when our soldiers were out in the open, in daylight, resting. It was the same in the city. They did cause harm. They could have been utterly destructive; they were not.

Now we are living in the occupation, and the bombers come again. Always at night. I think of them as the enemy because I don't know who they are. We have been taught to fold our warmer clothes and to place them on a chair next to our beds. We are always in the deep sleep of childhood when the howling of the sirens starts. The dogs hear the distant hum of the airplanes before any human can and their eerie howls are the first signal for those who are still awake or whose sleep is very light because they have children to protect. Long columns of searchlights slide in arcs, licking the night sky leisurely at first and then, as the sound increases, with more urgency, trying to spot the planes. And now sirens reach their furious crescendo warning that sounds like thousands of wolves gathering, lifting their heads to cry in the night. We hear our bedroom door opening quietly and then Baba's calm voice, "Don't be afraid, my children, we are in God's hand." We rise up, rubbing our eyes; we put on our outer clothes and walk downstairs rapidly to enter the dreaded basement that serves as a bomb shelter.

Thessaloniki is situated in an enviable location with its large, generous port and with a railroad station to facilitate transport from central Europe to the Mediterranean and from there to Africa. German installations and supply depots are the targets of the bombers, but the city is densely built and the bombs stray easily.

One night, after the all-clear, Daddy, together with a few other men, ventures to the empty street that is lit by the moonlight that no blackout can put out, and I hold on to his hand as he meets his brother, who lives a couple of apartment buildings to our right. The brothers whisper, wondering what the Allies had hit that night, how close the bombs had fallen, what tomorrow will bring. "Are we nearing the end? Are the Allies coming closer?" The eerie quiet of that night after the raids, the whispers, the strange blue light diffused in the street, lighting up the balconies and maybe the eyes that peer through the shutters—all that remains with me as a picture with a strange, otherworldly beauty, filled with mystery. I hold on to my Dad's hand and look all around me as if I suspect that this is a moment I will never forget. What is coming next? We then traipse upstairs, back to bed, maybe to dream of peace.

It was the Allies who flew overhead that night. When they hit an intended target, the all-clear was followed by the ra-ta-ta-tá of exploding ammunition. We were getting used to terrible and terrifying sounds.

❖ ❖ ❖

On Stratigou Doumbioti Street we knew everyone who lived across from us. Every balcony hid or revealed a story. I was familiar with every person who appeared on those balconies. Huge rocks covered the window of their basement. It served as the bomb shelter of that building, so the rocks were piled in the opening for protection. We city children who lacked yards with trees climbed on anything that looked hilly. One day one of those heavy rocks fell on my toe and smashed it. The pain was unbearable. For what seemed like weeks I had all kinds of home remedies applied to that wound. But it was nothing compared to my poor brother's frequent and dramatic accidents.

That same apartment building across the street must have held some special attraction because the boys congregated at its entrance. One morning, when only my grandmother and sisters were at home, the boys brought our brother Kostakis home covered in blood. He had cracked his forehead on the edge of the marble step of the building opposite ours. Where did so much blood come from? I remember my poor grandmother's despair and our own panic. Throughout those uncertain years, Kostakis would add to our misery by his accidents. Our main concern was to keep the worst from our mother, who doted on him—but we failed.

My brother's worst spanking happened after word reached us that he had been riding, "no-hands," downhill on St. Demetrius Street on his bicycle. There were no helmets or other imposed safety precautions on children those days. The terror that image of "no-hands" caused our mother was something that made all of us tremble. Afterward we were astounded that our brother survived the occupation but, emotionally, he barely survived our mother's death.

Light and Water

Even a sliver of light can dispel the darkness of a room; but a sliver of dark can never overwhelm the light.

—A childhood observation

Before falling asleep, in our darkened bedroom, I would focus on the thin strip of light that slipped underneath the door. It comforted me to know that my parents were just on the other side, talking. I started noticing the power of light, how even a little strip of it would enter to defeat the dark. I tried to imagine a strip of darkness entering a lighted room, but I knew that it would not make any difference to the light. I was very satisfied with that thought as sleep overtook me. During the daytime, however, we would all be aware of how limited our lives had become, how precious everything we had taken for granted was. Because the needs of the occupied don't matter to the occupiers. Electricity and running water were now memories of the past. We were becoming used to oil lamps on the table or hanging on the wall to light our way. At night we gathered around the dining table trying to decipher letters on paper by the soft light of the lamp. I learned to read and write in that semidarkness. Our little Niki, not yet four, was delighted by the huge shadows thrown on the wall. She moved her little hands and said in her sweet child's pronunciation, "Oh, look. Now all of you will say, 'My dear lady, what big hands you have!'"

All of us knew that water was precious, never to be wasted. The occupiers, who devoured everything, who stole every resource, allowed us an occasional hour of dripping water from the faucets, but during the worst of times all of us were enlisted in the carrying of buckets. In the summer, Daddy left the water in the clay pitchers, and we, fascinated by the miracle of science, watched them sweating. This process, we learned, worked like refrigeration, cooling the drinking water. As water poured from those clay pitchers, I listened for the gurgling sound that was so much like music. Water was more precious than gold. Many years later I would marvel at the ease with which Americans showered with unlimited water.

Waiting for the Allies

> . . . one thing this self-engrossed British society
> would not do "was to demean itself
> by any attempt to understand the people
> over whom it exercised its unsolicited guardianship."
>
> —Philip Sherrard, as quoted by Edmund Keeley in
> *Inventing Paradise*

As the hope of an Allied invasion increases, our country sinks further into despair, wanton destruction, and internecine fighting. Fascism and Nazism are familiar to us by now. We know they are bad. But we are not yet familiar with another word that will bring angst to our lives for five more years to come.

We have not yet been taught our recent history—only the ancient one and, closer to us, the War of Independence, our revolution against the Turks. But we are not being taught that the dictator Metaxas (who became a hero because of his resistance to Mussolini) had been personally selected in 1936 by the king—a man of German heritage who understood nothing of democracy, who escaped immediately after the day of occupation, who lived in Egypt and then England and was insistent upon returning to us as the Greek monarch after the war. Even as a child I found it grossly unfair and peculiar that the king and the government could escape all the destruction and horror of the war, living in safety either in Egypt or England, while the rest of us were in constant danger. The gall of all those who abandoned us was that they claimed all the positions of power when they returned after the German surrender. No wonder the Resistance remained bitter and angry for years to come.

The country was divided in two camps—those who wanted the king to come back—the royalists—and those who despised the thought of a Greek monarchy—the former Venizelists, now democrats. Fear of something called Communism made the royalists scream for the return of the king. Fear of Communism would turn even Churchill against the Greeks he had once praised for their bravery. Fear of Communism and interference from Russia and Yugoslavia would blanket the resistance movement as red while the Germans and the collaborationist government that worked with them took advantage of this fear to urge Greeks to fight against Greeks.

It was now mid-October 1944. Daddy had taken my brother to the store with him. It must have been another one of those days when schools couldn't open. The *agora* seemed deserted and Daddy started worrying that he had a ten-year-old child with him. They reached Valaoritou Street where the infamous Dángalos had his headquarters. Every corner was occupied by his armed henchmen, their weapons on the ready. With trepidation Daddy rolled up only one of the shop's metal shutters and, after hiding Kostakis inside, dared to stand outside, to examine the street. His fellow merchants were doing the same thing, whispering among themselves. Soon, one after the other, they started pulling downs the shutters again, and Daddy did the same.

Holding my brother's hand and hugging the walls, he started running from doorway to doorway to avoid the stray bullets. It took them a long time to return home while we stood with Mother at the balcony entrance watching for them. Everyone in the neighborhood seemed to be watching and waiting. The relief when the two returned home was overwhelming.

Later that afternoon, our father went downstairs to meet his older brother who lived nearby; they heard gunfire coming from the Upper City, where our grandparents lived. The two decided that we had to leave our homes, to check on our grandparents, and to spend the night with them in the hope that the fighting would soon move away from the Upper City. Taking whatever bedding we could carry, we climbed the hill to Grandfather's house. The rest of the brothers' families had the same idea, and soon we were all together in the safety and calm of our grandfather's prayers and faith. The adults discussed the rumors. "Everything has been mined. The Germans are blowing up all the bridges and every installation needed for the life of the city. They say that they will blow up the two main electric stations of Thessaloniki—the one at the depot and the one at St. Demetrius, near our homes."

Night is falling. We gather on the balcony and watch the dark night spreading over our beloved city. We can see the port, which we know has been mined. Now, every boat is burning and the jetty is exploding. Flashes of red illumine everything in horrible clarity. German mines, planted in the harbor, are going off like grotesque fireworks. The British and the Americans are bombing the enemy's stores of ammunition. The waterfront is in agony. Flaming pieces of ships shoot madly toward the sky. The earth and the sky become one in a monstrous conflagration. But the fury does not move uphill. We are safe. Later we learn that the Metropolitan of the city, together with other leaders, had given their promise to the retreating enemy that they would not be harmed by the populace. In the deal, the electric stations had been spared.

Our parents awakened us at dawn. We started downhill before even the vendors appeared in the streets. The narrow alleys and cobblestone paths of the old city were deserted. Quiet lay all around, ominous beneath the staccato drum motif of the explosions in the bay. Who hid in the doorways, lying in wait for departing Germans?

We reached Kassandrou street, the one parallel to our own. My father walked slightly ahead, carrying the baby in his right arm and holding my hand with his left. Immediately behind us, clutching the hands of my older brother and sister, came our mother.

We were almost home when, without warning, from behind an abandoned milk wagon, a man leaped and ran toward us. He was wearing the recognizable emblem of the guerrillas—down one shoulder and across his chest ran a bandoleer filled with cartridges. I still see him coming at us out of nowhere—a bearded, dusty figure with a flashing gun slung from his shoulder. I screamed but no sound emerged from my mouth. My father's hand tightened on mine, and then, the stranger's arms were around my father, hugging him, and in the Greek fashion, kissing him on each cheek.

Recognition, whispered conversation, a callused hand resting briefly on my hair, and urgency all around. He escorted us home to safety, and I kept thinking, "This, then, is a Communist." Once again, a friendship forged in the dangers of the frozen Albanian front had come to our rescue.

Day of Liberation

From the fierce edge of your sword I recognize you,
And from your eyes that quickly measure the earth.

—the first two lines of the "Hymn to Liberty,"
the Greek national anthem

—Author's translation.

My father's forty-first birthday fell on 30 October, the day of liberation. On that day, all of Thessaloniki unfurled into the blue and
white of our flag, the reflection of our Greek sea and sky. I stood on
tiptoe in our balcony, grasping the rails and bending my head side-
ways to feast my eyes on the clouds of waving flags adorning all the
other balconies on our street of side-by-side apartment buildings.
It was a street named after a Greek general, leading to the square of
the Administrative Building; its guard house had sheltered a but-
toned-down enemy face for all the years of my remembering. I
wondered who would be there today, now that the Germans were
gone. It was a day when we shed the drab of occupation to emerge
into the color of Greek freedom. Where had all those flags been
hiding? Even we children knew that possessing the *Galanólefki*,
the Blue-and-White, had been forbidden by the Nazi occupiers.
We hadn't seen our flag in nearly four years. Mother showed us
where she had hidden ours—at the bottom of the clothes chest. It
smelled of mothballs and camphor but it would air out as it flew
from the front balcony.

On that glorious day we were swimming in the recaptured joy of blue and white as before the war free people had been able to swim without fear in our blue sea. We children, jumping with excitement, told our parents that we couldn't stay inside on such a day, and they agreed. We joined the quarter-million of Thessaloniki's citizens in an excursion to defy all excursions, even in a city where the everlasting pastime was the evening promenade by the seashore. We poured into the streets. We laughed and played and watched the fear and worry disappear from our parents' brows.

I remember looking at my mother and thinking, *Mammá is so pretty!* It was later that I figured out the reason for this recognition—her open smile lit up her large, green eyes. I hadn't seen that light in a long while.

Our clothes were clean and pressed, though worn out from so many years of having only enough for survival. Like everyone else, the women of the city were thin, but they were dressed up in their high heels, their hair in elaborate, coiffed rolls as was the fashion of the time. My mother wore a small hat with a short, flirty veil. The memory of her holding my hand, bending toward me and laughing, entered my brain, burned itself there and remained to be recalled in the future decades of sorrow. On that day we walked, we ran, we talked to everyone around us while above us waved the blessed white and blue, the beloved colors of the Greek nation. It was a day of liberation. A day of unparalleled joy. The bands played the blood-throbbing rhythms of the Greek anthems, the words of our poet Solomos familiar on everyone's lips:

> *From the fierce edge of your sword I recognize you,*
> *and from your eyes that quickly measure the earth.*
> *We greet you, Liberty.*

The second stanza announces to Liberty that she has emerged from "the sacred bones of the Hellenes." What child would not believe it? We knew our history; we had swallowed our Homer and our mythology with our mother's milk. As the names of the fallen were uttered in the Ayia Sophia Square, our parents wept with this knowledge.

The euphoria lasted a very short while. On our return, as we reached Egnatia Street, we were met by another parade. Hundreds of men and women appeared, their arms and clenched fists in the air, yelling, "Kápa Kápa Épsilon!" the acronym of the Greek Communist Party. These people were not dressed in their finery like the rest of us but in ragged, quasi-military garb. A large group of young women who looked like university students were waving banners and yelling the acronym EPON, the youth corps of the Communist Party. It was all frightfully confusing.

The parades and the confusion continued while the *agora* remained closed for days. We couldn't even buy cheese or bread. We had gone from the agony of occupation, through a morning of joy, to chaos. New sounds filled the air. Across the street from us lived a medical student, one of those fascinating university people who attended school during the day and did secret things at night. With frightening regularity, he emerged on his balcony as darkness fell and his voice echoed through the megaphone: "Attention, attention, this is the voice of EAM." The acronym for the National Liberation Front became as familiar to us as the evening "goodnight." It hid within it danger and mystery and a kind of visceral excitement I felt but was then too young to know. Meetings, assemblies, and protests were constantly announced. We were drowning in acronyms.

We tried to ignore all of them until one day all citizens were called to celebrate victory at the Ayia Sophia square. Our parents decided that we should participate, together with our neighbors whose daughters played the piano and whom we admired. Thinking that this was a gathering for liberation, our parents were shocked to discover, when we arrived at the square, that it had been organized by the Communists who claimed that it was *their* resistance that had liberated Greece. My father and Mr. Iosiphidis showed their disgust by pulling us away to return home. Communism had become a fear-filled word. The strange parades continued.

"They are tobacco workers," I heard the grown-ups say, "labor unionists." But nobody bothered to explain why that allegiance was bad, and nobody tried to tell us what the word "communism" meant in itself. Only the connotation mattered and the connotation was bad. The protesters against the established government organized strikes that paralyzed the city. We could see them all clearly from our balconies. Their clothes bore evidence of their poverty—patches on elbows and knees, sleeves frayed and too short. At first we thought they were celebrating, but soon we knew that they were angry. One day it dawned on the Greeks: These are not parades; we are in the midst of a Communist uprising. The flags changed from blue and white to red.

A new phenomenon entered the street demonstrations—raised fists punching, punching the air. And a new color now appeared among the cheer of the blue and white—red banners with a yellow sign that even now makes me cringe because of the emotion surrounding it those long-ago days: the hammer and the sickle. It was all underscored by their singing of a sad Slavic song, "The Internationale," a strange replacement for the triumphant Greek anthems. "Who are they, Babá?" I asked. His answer must have been very cautious, because I don't remember it. But I do remember that this red color brought back the gloom that had covered us during the occupation. And then one day a new word with a loaded meaning entered my own vocabulary and some things started making sense even to a child.

It was a Monday—wash day. Our maid, Kyra Katina, was in the kitchen dipping the clothes into the boiling water, adding the bluing agent that would turn them white, another one of those grown-up paradoxes I was always examining. Mother was cooking the usual for a wash Monday—bean soup with its evocative aroma that meant warmth and comfort as it simmered on the stove in a sauce of olive oil, onion, celery root, tomato, and parsley. It was a rainy day, its gloom reflected on everyone's face. Daddy had come home for lunch, a deep worry line between his elegant brows. "What is going on in the city?" Mother must have asked because he said, "I'm afraid we are in the hands of Communists."

Ah, a new word. I knew instantly that it was bad. I read it in the tone of his voice—*Communists*. The men carrying the red, the hammer and the sickle—they were bad. Their angry fists punching the air—they were bad. What had happened to the joy of the day of liberation? We drew close to our mother, touching her skirt, close to our father, touching his familiar back. *Don't let the fear come back into your eyes, don't start looking sad again.* But I didn't say it aloud. At least now the fear had a name. There was a clear separation that made sense to the child—good from bad.

For us children, this separation between good and bad was somehow comforting. We knew whom to support. The king should come back; that's what the frightened parents longing for peace, longing "for law and order," were saying, echoing our allies, the Brits. It was the fear of Communism that lay underneath the ridiculous desire to have a king. Because in those days, everything that was not red was good. The greatest horror fell on the children of peasants as it had done through centuries upon centuries of invaders on this blood-soaked Greek soil. The Communist guerrillas kidnapped children from their villages, we read in the papers. Carried behind the Iron Curtain, into Yugoslavia, they would be raised as passionate Communists—just as the Turks of old had done to Greek children they abducted, the ones who grew up to become the vicious, feared Janissaries. In the land of myths, the myths persisted.

Communism was bad. But why? Who were these people called Communists? They had been in the mountains fighting the Nazis, blowing up bridges together with our British allies, who now were also fighting against us. Once they were heroes. Yet, the tragedy was that when resistance fighters attacked or abducted one German soldier, whole villages would pay in retribution. Heroic acts brought horrid consequences. Why was the world so confusing? Daddy, a patient teacher, tried to explain: the courageous people who had fought the Germans were the partisans, heroes of the nation, like the *klefts* in the war of independence from the Turks more than a century before. But among them were others who wanted to get rid of the Germans in order to take control of Greece for the sake of Russia. Russia was red; Russia was Communist; Russia was bad. *Are our soldiers good?* we wondered. Stories of horrors committed by both sides reached us daily.

Daddy lowered the basket from the balcony every morning for the newspaper that brought us news of the past night's tragedies in the villages. Brother was killing brother; echoes of Nazi atrocities were now being committed by our own. Daddy would read the headlines right there as we munched on the *koulouria*, the traditional sesame bread baked in a slender circle; the bread, together with the bad news, had been added to our basket by the vendor who started work early, walking the streets, carrying his wares. Nearly everything needed for survival those days was carried in people's arms or backs and sold in the streets—even bad news. Our father was careful to let us know that it was not only the guerrillas who committed atrocities; the right-wing Security Battalions did also. The news reinforced an uncomfortable knowledge: The good were not always good; the bad were not always bad. And who was good?

One night, weeks after the day of liberation, we are again gathered around the table for Daddy to read us the nightly story from the Bible before bedtime. We had spent the previous years of our childhood getting ready for the bomb shelter, in case the sirens would sound to alert us of the coming of the Allies in airplanes that dropped bombs on the Nazi installations of the city, and sometimes on the Greeks. On this night, instead of sirens, a new noise explodes in our apartment building. The stairwell with its terrazzo flooring is a huge echo chamber. Hobnailed boots run up and down, doors open and close, frightened voices from neighbors rise and fall—and then a kick on our own door. Our father opens it, and there stands a fully armed soldier, demanding to search the small apartment—for an escaped *andarte*, he says, the Greek word for guerrilla. Terror on everyone's face, loss of control, utter confusion: How can anyone come in to hide in such a small place? The boots go to the balcony to check if one can jump from there to another building, then move to the bedrooms to open the small wardrobes. When they leave—how many have entered?—we seem like a different family. Something has been desecrated. I suspect that these are the right-wing killers, perhaps no better than the Communists.

One hot day, the Greek sun burning everything white, Babás is late coming home for lunch. The city is very quiet in the stillness of siesta, so the gunfire sounds loud and persistent. We watch our mother's worried face. The shutters to the front balcony are already closed but, curious as ever, I open them a crack to look outside. Nothing stirs in the deserted street below, but the air is filled with danger. A dog barks, but even that sound is hesitant. I feel the intense heat enveloping the balcony. Now a lone man appears. He is limping, his white shirt covered in blood. He is moving down the middle of the empty street in a strange, half bent way, holding on to his arm. Is he being chased? But if he is, why is he in the middle of the street? Is that a gun in his good hand? Before I can find out, I am pulled sharply away from the shutters. I am still wondering what happened to that man.

When my father finally appears, he is out of breath as he describes that it took him hours to walk from his store to the house. A fifteen-minute walk had turned to hours as he moved from doorway to doorway to wait, to avoid men with guns running through the city. No one knows which side is being chased, who is doing the chasing.

And so opened that huge chasm between the right and the left, the good and the bad. It would be bloody and barbarous and only a Thucydides would have understood it enough to describe it equitably as he had done with earlier civil wars, the Peloponnesian.

❊ ❊ ❊

During that fateful decade, I learned that small nations are pawns in the hands of much more powerful nations; that the poor are considered dangerous when they demand their rights in an unjust society; that violence hurts the most vulnerable, not necessarily those who practice it; and that the oppressed soon become oppressors. My hatred for war and my compassion for children living in war and poverty date from that day of liberation.

The Foreign Involvement

Although it was not my business as a soldier, I humbly stressed that the sooner the King openly stated that he would not set foot in Greece until he was asked for by the common vote of the people, the better would be the chances of internal peace for the country.

—Brigadier E. C. W. Myers, SOE, reporting to Cairo from the Greek mountains

Two Brits started coming to our church and to our home now that the Allies were back in our land. Our streets smelled of aromatic tobacco smoked by soldiers and sailors who dressed and behaved differently from our own. There were the ruddy, smiling New Zealanders and Australians, appearing so brave and self-confident to us devastated and malnourished Greeks. There was the flirty dark beret of French soldiers and the jauntiness of the burgundy British berets, our closest allies who had returned to a Greece they had fled after the Germans invaded. They were still welcome, though terrible fights took place between their forces and Greek civilians in the streets of Athens during the December after liberation. It was all so confusing. We knew that when the Germans were invading us, many Greeks had risked their own lives to hide British soldiers until they could escape through the ports. How could the Brits turn against us?

During the occupation, a number of courageous British commandoes of the secret SOE (Special Operations Executive), its role revealed after the war, had parachuted onto the gorges and roofs of our wild, snowcapped mountains, risking life and limb. A few of them, steeped in Greek history and philosophy at Oxbridge, worked together with the resistance against the Nazis. Others immediately disapproved of the hard-headed Greek leaders who refused to obey British orders. In the months following the liberation, paranoia against Communism was infecting the Brits as bitterly as their justified hatred of Nazism had a few months before. Churchill, who had been such an inspiration against Hitler and who had praised the courageous Greek army against Mussolini, now turned against the Greeks, even urging his soldiers to fight them in the streets of Athens. With great stubbornness and the arrogance that characterized him, he wanted the king to return to Greece, but the resistance was adamantly opposed to his return. And so the civil war started.

The Americans were altogether different. Young and healthy, they liked our city and its waterfront, but they could not hold their ouzo. It was terribly embarrassing to see them on the *paralia*, our waterfront promenade, so obviously drunk. The Greeks, still quite puritanical, were shocked at the Americans, but that didn't keep them from considering them the luckiest people on earth.

Harry Vernon and Neville Sampson, our Brits, came to worship with us and as usual Mother fed them. I remember how pretty the fried eggs, sunny-side-up, looked on the plate; they called the evening meal "tea" and we thought it very funny. My mother was very fond of Neville, who looked so young and blonde and British. It was a very sad day when they had to say goodbye to us. Daddy and I walked them downstairs to the exit of the building. I didn't understand everything they said, but I surmised (or maybe Dad explained later) that they were leaving Greece because the Americans were now responsible for us.

Stalin and Churchill had made an agreement between them: Stalin, despite the strong local Communist uprising, would not claim Greece; Churchill made it clear that it belonged to the British sphere. And he, of course, would be hands-off on the countries Stalin soon devoured, the countries that would become hidden behind the Iron Curtain. Again, listening to my father, I had the feeling that Greece was not of value in herself; that the Great Powers could move us like pawns for their purposes and national interest. The economy was in shambles, the land devastated, and we were continually being humiliated while one government after another came and went without improving our situation.

To our own family, the war and its many daily deprivations, struggles, and even terrors brought on tragic results. All those tears and agonies and lack of proper nourishment our mother suffered on behalf of her husband and children chipped away at an already fragile body and the old menace returned.

My Magical Year That Wasn't

> God may not play dice with the universe,
> but something strange is going on with
> the prime numbers.
>
> — Paul Erdös, a Hungarian mathematician,
> wordplay on Einstein's famous saying

It was meant to be magical, that ninth year of my life. But its end proved to be sad and frightening beyond my imagining.

Nine was *my* magic number. Steeped in biblical stories, I knew about the good magic of three and seven and even of twelve, but no one had singled *nine* as magical. I was going to be the one to do it. Enneagram hadn't been thought of yet, so the number hadn't entered anyone's consciousness.

And here I digress, trapped by words and their etymology, as usual. *Ennéa*. Do non-Greek speakers recognize it immediately as nine, the way my mind does? And *gram*: Definitely not the weight measurement in this context, it means either line—*grammê*—or letter and writing—*grámma*. Nine lines, nine personality types. I have never taken the test. And this has to do with the year I had thought would be magical.

> I am completing the ninth year of my life. I was
> born on December 9. I lived on Number 9, Stratigou
> Doumbioti Street, in the heart of Thessaloniki, so this
> memory is of my birthday. How could it not be magical

for me? Now we are walking home, the three of us.
My older sister is thirteen. Kostas, much older, is walking between us and we are holding him *engagé*. We had
adopted that French word into Greek; women loved to
walk *engagé*, their hands in the crook of the man's arm.
We are laughing as we climb the street toward home.
The reason for the laughter cannot be recalled.

Kostas was our family's favorite friend, handsome enough to be
admired by every woman who passed us by. His older sister was our
beloved aunt Ida, whose compassion had saved our home during the
war. Why he was walking with us I don't know. Maybe Mammá had
invited him to lunch.

The sound that stays alive in my memory even today
is our laughter. Why were we happy? It had to be something personal. In our wider world, the war had ended
and what came to be called the first round of the civil
war was over. We didn't know then that a second one,
much longer and more brutal, awaited us.

As we try to walk in rhythm, I am chattering about
the magic of number nine and Kostas is impressed with
my cleverness. Doritsa, much shier than I, is speaking
more rarely. Kostas is amused, and as I gaze at him side-
ways I admire his elegant profile, that straight nose that
adds such an aristocratic touch to his smiling lips.

Maybe we had enough cause for laughter. I hold on to
that memory, the spot on Venizelou Street, right before
it climbed more steeply to pass by the marbled courtyard across from the Ministry and its few pine trees.

We used to pull the pine needles and, pressing each sharp end into the tender root, we entwined them, making chain links to wear around our necks. We loved smelling of pine.

Now we are inside the apartment and all laughter ends. Daddy emerges from our parents' bedroom. His face is troubled, and I read fear on it. He pulls Kostas in with him. Mammá is in bed. I think the doctor is inside also, but the people no longer matter. What matters is that a medicinal smell falls on us like a cloud and drenches us with dread. We look at each other. No one remembers it's my birthday; even I have forgotten. "What's the matter with Mammá?" we ask each other, knowing already that it's a terrible question, that the answer will contain terror. I hear the words, the ominous words: "She coughed up blood." The hated word, tuberculosis, is unspoken, but we know in our bodies what that blood means. From that day on, the sound of a deep cough would accompany my days and nights. In the middle of the night I would think: I hope she coughs it all up, so it will stop. Will it stop? My older sister answers a sad *no*.

On the day that was to have ushered in a new year for me, how did I know that we were entering a time of impending doom? We tiptoed around in a world that changed that minute. There would be three more years of unbearable suffering for her and a sad uncertainty for us, but on my tenth birthday, magic disappeared from my world.

The Gift of the Imagined

You can do more with a castle in a story than with the
best cardboard castle. . ..

—C. S. Lewis, *Surprised by Joy*

The first summer of Mamma's illness descends
on Thessaloniki, the merciless heat reflecting from
asphalt and concrete. Those who can do so escape
to neighboring villages. The poor peasants move their
families to the ground floor and rent the upstairs to city
folk. They make enough from the rent to survive the
winter—survival, after all, has been their game for
centuries.

1945. It is a strange summer, one of suspended
life, an expectancy in the air, and we are unsure of
whether it is ominous or benevolent. The Nazis are
gone, the civil war has stopped for a while, so we now
breathe. The summer house is on a low hill, bedrooms
and living room upstairs, the kitchen below. The stairwell has thin, unstable railings and I love playing there,
my legs around these railings. One afternoon one of
them breaks and I tumble to the lower steps. So much
for allowing our mother to live in peace. On another
day, I am in the kitchen alone, and though I am usually
an obedient child, I now do what Daddy has forbidden;

I play with a sharp knife, the one reserved for slicing bread, and make a spectacular cut between my thumb and index finger. That day, the doctor has to be called. I dread what Daddy will say. These are two minor memories from a pleasant, quiet summer for us children. But the next scene is much more vivid and enduring because it has cosmic implications.

In our immediate family the future is already under lengthening shadows. My father has told us that Mammá suffers from bronchitis, because even children under ten know that the other word means death. His patrician features—high forehead and elegant, straight nose—are under a perpetual cloud, a quizzical look in his eyes, a groove beginning between the brows. Is it possible, the eyes say, that my four children will be left motherless?

The entire Katsarka clan has survived the war intact. Our mother will be the first casualty. For now, Daddy gives her what she needs—an airy spot on the hills, her children with her, and the sanitarium, which until the end she refuses to enter, nearby.

Daddy leaves early each morning for the city, a large covered basket in his hand. Her returns each evening on the pitiful buses that have surfaced after the war, his basket loaded with goods from the *agora*. Despite the uncertainty and illness, it is a good summer. I am beginning to pay attention to the earth. The flowering thistles have a rough beauty that is unruly and unexpected. We chase butterflies on the long climbs of the bare scorched hills with the dizzying aroma of dried herbs under our feet. The cows, skinny and spare, leave early in the morning to graze on what green is left on the ravaged earth, their bells low and mellifluous when they return at dusk, the smell of burning twigs in the air as the village women cook their meals.

On 6 August Daddy returns early, always an occasion to celebrate, and we sit on the balcony floor while he sips his coffee. Our parents talk in quiet voices as we play at their feet, absently listening.

"They dropped the atom bomb on Japan, Persephóne," he tells my mother, and though the phrase means nothing to me, I hear its utterance, paying attention to the awe in Dad's voice, and the look in Mother's eyes, the "What does this mean for my children?" look. "Atom" is the word I catch, and it seems strange that it causes fear, this familiar Greek word, átomo, which in our language means a person, an individual. How is it that the individual has such awesome power? Why does Daddy sound so foreboding? Japan is far, far away.

A storm is coming up. I smell the damp in the atmosphere. Across the narrow valley I see the clouds gather. They cover the hills on the other side of the village, making them invisible, as though they no longer exist. It's the first time I notice clouds as a wall, a total means of concealment. In the city clouds are only high up, in the sky; here they descend like the breath of the gods from Mt. Olympos. I feel expectant and free. Something is brewing in my mind. Caves open up behind the clouds like a "Welcome home" from a lonely little girl who now smiles and beckons me to come in. Without moving I run to her. "Do you have toys?" I ask her.

"Toys?" she repeats as if the word is new and strange to her. "I have paper and pencil and I write stories."

"May I play this game with you?" I ask, and she gives me her paper.

I am finding the escape of the imagined. "Babá, please, I need a notebook." The magic is continuing: Daddy gives a few drachmas to my brother, who accepts the request and runs to the kiosk. He brings back a red notebook with faint blue lines and in it I write my first story.

I have found my way out of the hovering darkness. Every 6 August that has rolled around since then, I have thought of that afternoon in an inconspicuous Greek village. I have remembered the children of Hiroshima and Nagasaki who did not get the chance to escape the darkness. And I remember that ever since that day in August, it hovers, hovers above all the world's children.

The Other Family

> For this reason a man shall leave
> his father and mother and be joined to his wife,
> and the two shall become one flesh.
>
> —Matthew 19:5

The memories of our mother's healthy years become overshadowed by the fear and worry of the sick time. Every now and then they slip through and I am filled with sorrow and regret that I did not get to know her better. We are not even certain of what her last name was nor of her exact birthday.

She never turned the poor away, those who came to our door begging for bread or drachmas. The only ones from her part of the world familiar to us were the two aunts, sisters of our maternal grandmother, who died when Mammá was only four. When we visited them, we usually spent time with Aunt Anna, who lived with her husband and son upstairs while the other sister lived downstairs. I think that by the time we met her, the second aunt was a widow. We knew that our own mother was the only girl in her family, the youngest child after the birth of six sons. All the children had been given ancient names—Odysseus and Achilles are the only two I remember—and of course, the most mythological and rather ominous was that of our own mother: Persephóne. It seems that all of Epiros, that wild western part of Greece where they were born, still carried the deep memories of the ancients. For centuries, Epiros, bordering the Ionian Seas and cut off from the rest of Greece by the long mountain range of the Pindos, was isolated and unknown. Alexander the Great's mother, the equally wild Olympias, was born in that region. The names were familiar to us and their stories did not seem strange.

In mythology, Persephóne was the beloved daughter of Démetra, the earth goddess, the giver of wheat. Lovely Persephóne was abducted by Hades and taken down to the underworld. Démetra's motherly grief brought on the dying of the earth in autumn, the final death in winter. But every six months, Persephóne was allowed to return from the underworld, bringing with her the resurrection of springtime and the warmth of summer. The myth was part of my childhood. The ancient names haunted me. Why did this poor family from Filiátes give the children names of such ancient lore? They, who probably had no schooling, named them after mythological characters. Where did the knowledge come from? In that distant, poor, wildly beautiful western province, did the myths live in communal memory? Did they know that the river Styx was in their region? That Persephóne was worshiped there, and that the entrance to the underworld, to Hades, was in Epiros also? The questions persist.

My mother's brother, Achilles, visited us in Thessaloniki and Mother mended his clothes and fed him while he was there. But this too remains a vague memory, together with the nephew who also came to see her. To my shame, we were all so focused on the Katsarka clan and our Protestant identity that we ignored the other relatives. We had created this "in group" that left out all those who did not belong within its circle.

The tragedy of my mother's family started early. My maternal grandmother's early death affected the whole family. Her husband remarried and the stepmother's lack of love caused the boys to emigrate from Epiros. So the two aunts brought the little orphaned Persephóne to Thessaloniki with them. When I became sentimental about them, my older sister rebuked me by reminding me that they had brought her to be their maid. I never asked questions about that because I was so grateful that in the city she met my father.

Her schooling in an American institution was short lived, but there she first heard the words "Protestant" and "evangelical" and there she learned the hymnody that would become so much a part of her short life. In her teens, out of necessity, she started work in a milliner's shop. The owner was a Jewish woman who employed three young girls of her own faith and a sole Greek girl by the name of Persephóne.

The atelier was in the Kolombo *stoa,* the short arcade that cut through from Egnatia to Valaoritou Street. The young Vassilis Katsarkas had his shop at the entrance of that *stoa* and there he first noticed the pretty, short, and circumspect seventeen-year-old with the huge green eyes, bent over her felt cloths and her colorful feathers and threads. She responded to his admiring stares by smiling sweetly. They fell in love in the manner of fictional characters in eighteenth-century novels—by exchanging glances. He was already twenty-six, but in the claustrophobic atmosphere of the tiny evangelical community he had never been near girls. He was an innocent who had never heard of women's menstruation. He first heard the word "brassiere" when he was doing his basic training and the officer laughed at him: "You, Katsarka. What world do you live in?" But worse than all of this ignorance was his conviction, taught at home, that one "should not yoke oneself to nonbelievers." So, knowing himself to be falling helplessly in love, he was tortured by this conviction: Persephóne did

My parents' formal engagement photo. 1930.

not belong to the Protestant community; therefore, in their mind, she was a nonbeliever.

The four young milliners had to walk through the *stoa* to take their daily breaks. Vassilis noticed how quiet and modest she was by comparison to the other girls. One of the men dared to tease her one day and, as he reported to my father later, she almost hit him with her bag. "She's a wild one," the man said, and my father liked her even more. But when he told his parents of his falling in love with someone outside their closed community, their response was deep sadness and disappointment. His older brother, known for being priggish, wrote him a long letter castigating him for dishonoring the family. Poor Vassilis. Yet, Providence interfered in the guise of fashion.

Felt hats, popular at the time, needed a couple of holes on the side so that the wearer would not suffer from perspiration and heat.

Persephóne now found an excuse to bring hats to Vassilis's shop because these holes needed capsules to keep them from unraveling. Vassilis took his time stapling them on so that he could exchange conversation with the pretty girl who blushed so readily. So he learned of her orphaned state and of her aunts in Thessaloniki. Because of his family's disapproval, he tried to suppress his feelings, but they blossomed to an unspoken passion.

A whole year passed; Persephóne, losing hope, asked for a transfer to another shop, and Vassilis slipped into depression. His parents, seeing him in such a lovesick condition, relented. His brother, always condescending, wrote him another letter (even though they both still lived in the same parental home), telling him they were all sick of watching his suffering. Arrangements were made. A fellow merchant in the *stoa* and his wife, acting as matchmakers, visited the aunts and uncles and, as was the custom, asked for Persephóne's hand on Vassilis's behalf. The formal engagement was set for the following Sunday. The aunts, together with their husbands and the matchmaking couple, accompanied young Persephóne, eighteen years of age, to the Katsarka home. There, with the whole family surrounding them, they exchanged the engagement bands—the gold rings worn on the fourth finger of the left hand and changed to the right hand on the day of the wedding. For the first time Vassilis touched the hand of the girl he had adored from afar for longer than a year, and my grandparents finally set eyes on the pretty, modest, and sweet Persephóne. She met with their approval. On the following Wednesday, the young couple took a long walk together, unchaperoned. There, in the wooded park, he dared kiss her on the cheek. She laughed at him. "This is not how engaged people kiss, Vassilaki," using the affectionate form of his name. And to his amazement and delight, he felt her lips on his own.

They had to wait until the firstborn brother was married before they could have a wedding of their own a week later. Vassilis and Persephóne were married on 6 December 1931. And so started my mother's involvement in the *ekklesia* and the Katsarka family. She helped my grandmother in all housework, earning admiration for her skills and cleanliness. In their house church she learned the hymns and scripture lessons with her quick and agile mind. Her lovely soprano blended with our grandmother's as they sang hymns together.

After the weddings of all five sons, it dawned on this ridiculously close-knit family that they could not all live together in peace, and the couples finally started creating their own households. But they stayed within walking distance, always in one another's company, until the 1950s and my own departure for America.

⌗ ⌗ ⌗

I am aware that I know very little about my mother. I do know that she kept us clean and dressed in our finest always. Everything was washed and ironed to perfection. She was immensely proud of her husband and her four children and she could be a tigress when any of us was threatened. But I know so little about who she truly was or could have become. This doesn't keep me from agonizing over the question: Was it the precariousness of her childhood years that eventually caused her death? She could have beaten the disease; she could have survived. But something in her character made her incapable of living away from us and from our father, even if that absence meant that she could have lived. Tuberculosis demands rest, quiet, good food, and more rest in a sanitarium environment—things she rejected. The regret over this basic weakness in her personality caused me and my siblings endless sorrow and repeated discussions. One of our aunts by marriage had a sister who had contracted tuberculosis. She went to the hospital for an operation that was practiced at that time—the removal of a rib and surgery on the infected part of the lung—and she survived to live into her seventies. Why couldn't our mother have allowed the same procedure on herself?

Our father tried in desperation. He took her to Athens during the civil war, a time when only travel by sea was possible. All the evangelical community in the capital promised them their support when Dad accompanied her to the hospital that specialized in this surgery. But our mother never stopped her pathetic weeping and made it absolutely clear that she would not stay there. Even a lengthy pastoral visit by the most beloved leader of the community, Kostas Matellinos, failed to change her mind. At the end, she forced my father to bring her back to Thessaloniki, afraid as he was that she would sign herself out and get lost in Athens.

I was on the balcony sweeping the tiles, ready to sit on my little chair, to read my book in peace. My grandmother was cooking and the other children were getting used to the idea that a miracle would happen and Mammá would return home if not well, at least much better. I put the broom up and turned toward the street. I saw my mother coming around the corner, walking toward the building's front door; she looked up at me and smiled, but I felt dread coursing through me. I knew that moment that the end would come for her and for us all. I don't know why the premonition was so strong. I ran to the kitchen to tell Yiayia and the kids, "Mammá is back. She didn't stay in Athens." I could tell immediately that they also understood what this return meant. We went to open the door, our smiles forced. Mammá looked happy and excited about the sea voyage because dolphins had followed the ship, frolicking and filling everyone aboard with delight. But for us, the beginning of the end filled us with bewilderment. For our father, the tragic failure of that trip haunted him from then on.

Family Lore

All sorrows can be borne
if you put them into a story
or tell a story about them.

—Isak Dinesen, as quoted by Hannah Arendt in
The Human Condition

My father was tender with us, especially with his girls, and utterly devoted to our mother, whom he loved with a passion that never abated. The years of her illness were his personal tragic journey, one that he could share only with his parents. Tuberculosis was such a dreaded disease that even Dad's brothers could not be a comfort to him. We were children, but even we were fully aware of his loneliness and isolation. We too became careful and withdrawn, afraid to ask questions that would add to his sorrow. The journals my father kept of his wife's illness are heartbreaking even now, seventy years after her death and suffering.

My father's hands are what I remember the most; they were always clean and dry, never sweaty, and he insisted on our having clean hands too. He held ours wherever we walked and his wife always had her hand in the crook of his elbow. He loved white collars on his girls' blouses and dresses. And he washed our faces and combed our hair every morning. He smelled of lemony cologne and I don't ever remember him unshaved. At night he read us stories from the Bible, believing them literally, something that would cause friction between us in my adulthood. He was a man of unfailing faith and prayer and nothing in his life negated his beliefs, though doubts and questions must have assailed him during the tragic years. He emerged still faithful to the end.

Yet, he had been dealt a great injustice: he was pulled out of school entirely too early. Because his second son was a good-looking boy with a very quick mind, my grandfather decided that higher schooling would be a great temptation, that he would lose his son to the great tempter. The teacher went to Grandfather's shop to tell him how bright his son Vassilis was, how he should make every effort to send him on to higher education, but my grandfather decided to do the exact opposite. I regret that I never had the opportunity to question my grandfather about his preposterous thinking.

So, after learning to read and write, still with a fevered desire for further studies, my father was deprived of what he loved most next to his family. The young boy was heartbroken, but even though he was bitterly aware of the injustice, he never questioned his father's decision. Instead, he started reading everything that came his way. He devoured newspaper editorials, absorbing their style, and grew up with a faultless command of the Greek language. But throughout his life he used more *katharevousa*, the artificial, purist language, than *demotiki*, the popular, spoken one. And here is a digression.

After the 1821–1829 War of Independence, the new Greek state didn't know whether it belonged to the ancient past or to the nineteenth-century present, when Greeks had been under the Ottoman yoke for four hundred years. In order to honor their ancestors, the new Greek nation created an artificial, purist language that still exists in newspapers and formal discourse. It took the genius of writers and poets like Palamas, Kazantzakis, Seferis, Elytis, and others to bring the language of the people, the demotic tongue, to the writing of literature. This pulsating, throbbing, pliable, and living language was rejected by the ecclesiastical and political intelligentsia but espoused by the literati and spoken by the people. My father never quite adapted to the demotic in his writing and preaching but did exceptionally well with the *katharevousa*, much to our amusement and teasing. He was a true autodidact.

He spent every free hour studying—reading every biblical exegesis that agreed with that of literalists, studying the Bible itself, and reading the encyclopedia. Learning English was the one good thing that happened in his education, a gift that became quite important in our future household.

My earliest memories of singing include, "It's a Long Way to Tipperary"—a word I thought wonderfully funny—"Bringing in the Sheaves," "Jesus Loves Me," and other English songs and hymns. Daddy sang them with great gusto. While telling us stories of his life, he would break out into song in various languages—a ditty sung by Bulgarians in Adrianople; a song by the Turks of his neighborhood; a Greek fighting song full of rhymes and puns. Despite his extreme dislike of Turks as a national entity, he quoted their proverbs with admiration. He loved to imitate the song of the *muezzin*, heard in his Adrianople childhood and never forgotten.

As was the prevalent custom of the day, he stereotyped ethnicities, but he had the grace to remember and honor individual persons within those nationalities. He remembered the neighbor woman next door in Adrianople who observed Ramadan with her husband; longing to have children of her own, she would open the door of her fenced-in yard after the fast to offer delicious pilaf and other delicacies to the Christian children next door.

When the Second Balkan War ended in 1913 with the Turks victorious, the so-called New Turks started a campaign of extinction against the six million Armenians and Greeks who had lived in the old Byzantium for centuries. It was now Turkey and everyone who was not a Turk was an infidel. The Greeks and Armenians had been the educated and merchant class of the region. Now people who had never done much physical work, who had taught in schools and had sat in offices, found themselves recruited for slave labor, breaking rocks for road building and other humiliating activities. Armenians and Greeks of the Pontus area were sent on long, forced marches toward deep Asiatic Turkey. Most of them died on the way in a genocide never acknowledged by the Turks. In the western parts, in Thrace (Thraki), where Adrianople was located, the people lived in constant fear of a knock on the door, of being force-marched to their death. Many of the Greek families had already left for the motherland. My grandfather corresponded with friends, asking questions about life and possibilities in Mother Greece. The most persuasive voices, however, were those of Turkish friends and customers, most of them civil or military employees. These men, not fellow Greeks, were the ones who told him that the purpose of the New Turks was to exterminate the Greek population of Turkey. And my grandfather, to his credit, believed them and made the necessary arrangements and the painful decision to uproot his nine-member family, to make them refugees in the motherland.

I remember as a child hearing this story and imagining the thrill but not the difficulties and dangers associated with such a decision. I was only glad that they had escaped and found a home in our beloved Thessaloniki. I now read my father's writings about that journey and marvel that the eleven-year-old boy noticed so much, absorbed so much, and was able sixty years later to describe sights and sounds and feelings with such vividness. When I read what he has written, I see the Turkish inspector on the train from Adrianople to the Polis examining their papers and I hear him asking in derision, "You are going to Greece, eh? If you ever get there. . . ." I see the two older boys hiding under the blankets so as not to see the mean expression on that inspector's face, not to hear the implication of the words. The days of waiting in thrilling Constantinople until a Greek ship would appear to take them to freedom pass before my eyes as the little boy goes to the port to watch the unending movement of sea and crowds. I listen to the sounds aboard the ship as they waited on it for three days before they could sail away. I catch a glimpse of the great Galata Bridge opening to let the larger ships through, and finally the slow gliding through to the sea of Propontis. And above all, with those nine members of my family that years later I would get to know, I see the joy of the Greeks aboard the ship and hear the sounds of their singing and dancing. They are free, they have escaped, they are going home to Greece, a land they have never seen but have dreamed of. The little boy—who was to become my father—sees and shares in this joy of liberation. But underneath it all he also hears the lament for all those who were lost in the vast spaces of Asiatic Turkey, of the Armenians and Greeks who were marched to their death. He senses what I would sense years later—that under the joy and the dancing there runs in the Greek psyche the awareness of human tragedy and pain. The theater masks of comedy and tragedy are always pictured together.

The year was 1914, so within months after their arrival in Thessaloniki, World War I would affect all the inhabitants of the ancient city. It was at that time filled with thousands of Jews and their culture and with the remnants of the Ottomans, with their mosques and minarets, their *calderims*—the narrow, cobblestone streets with their characteristic, overhanging upper stories of their dwellings—and the many cafés where the Turks of Thessaloniki drank their coffee and smoked the *nargile* pipes. The impressionable and romantic eleven-year-old felt at home among them, in that Oriental atmosphere that reminded him of his beloved Adrianople. The difference was that the dominating Turks of his mother city were now the subservient Muslims of the Greek city. He loved it all, especially the leafy walks, the plane trees, and the public cisterns with the blessed running water.

The home my grandfather rented for his family had been built by a rich Turk who, unable to live in a city where the Greeks now had the upper hand, left for the east. The annual rent was eighteen gold sovereigns, a serious amount at that time. The store he rented on Egnatia Street cost him twenty-eight gold sovereigns a year. This multicultural city had twice as many Jews as Greeks, plus many Turks, Bulgarians, and other ethnicities, making up a population totaling a hundred and fifty thousand people. Because the Jews owned the banks, the wholesale and retail businesses, and were highly observant of their religious practices with their many synagogues and schools, they controlled the life of the *agora*. Saturday was sacrosanct, with most stores closed for the day. Yet Sunday was market day, the day the villagers came to the city to buy and sell, a very profitable time for business owners. So my grandfather was confronted by a dilemma. On Saturday, with the market tightly closed, he did no business. Sunday for him was the Day of the Lord, reserved for worship and rest. He chose, with no personal struggle, to obey what he believed was required of him. His fellow Greeks told him he was missing out on a day that equaled all the rest of the week in business, but though he lost money he never yielded. It was that faith and a strength of character and conviction that were his hallmark, and we grew up knowing that he was a man of unbreakable integrity.

Meanwhile Europe was at war. The great statesman Venizelos wanted Greece to align with the Entente—Great Britain, France, and Russia—but the king, with familial ties to Germany, wanted Greece to remain neutral. Thus the great rift between the liberal democrats and the royalists opened in the country, never again to close, as the royalists transformed into the right wing. By 1916, Thessaloniki was crowded with troops from the many French and British colonies. And on the home front, tragedy hit the family with the death of the beloved twelve-year-old Katerina, the only girl in the family. My grandmother never laughed again.

As the war progressed Thessaloniki's empty lots and land were covered with thousands of tents housing British and French soldiers. Remarkable to a child's eye were the enormous square-shaped tents that served as hospitals. The great National Schism widened as Greece was pulled into the warring factions.

And then came 5 August 1917. A poor woman in one of the makeshift refugee neighborhoods of the city lit a fire to heat water for the weekly wash. On that hot day, the fierce vardar wind was blowing through Thessaloniki. She did not notice that a burning piece of wood jumped to the neighboring yard. Most of the Turkish-built homes were wooden and the wind carried the fire with incredible swiftness through the huts of the poor to the commercial part of the city, to the waterfront and the famous White Tower, which had stood on the edge of the sea as part of the city walls and fortification since the fifteenth century. On that August day the city was desperately dry, for it had not rained for five months. Because of the war, the city's water supply was being diverted for the needs of the hundred thousand foreign troops whose leaders refused to make it available for firefighting. At that time, the water needs of the populace were served only from wells; in the evenings they waited their turn at the public cisterns to fill up for drinking water. Here is a rare eyewitness report of that famous fire from my own father, fourteen-year-old Vassilis:

I had been working at my father's shop that summer. At 2:00 o'clock I went across the street to the café to fill my clay pitcher with water. I saw a black cloud moving from the Upper City toward the center. I ran to call Father as other merchants appeared on the street to see what was happening. Father and I tried to determine if the fire was near our home, but it was Saturday and we had to finish the shoes that were due that evening for the customers to pick up. Now Menelaos [the third son] arrived, frightened: "Father, the fire has reached Ayia Ekaterini's church and Mother wants you to come home immediately. She is very worried." Father left and I remained together with our one employee. It took a long time for Father to return together with my older brother. They told us that the fire had changed direction and was now heading toward Egnatia Street where our own shop was located. Because of the tall buildings on Egnatia we could see only the smoke but not the flames. I started urging Father to gather whatever was of value because we would lose it all to the fire. Father, however, thought that the cement buildings would stop the fire. Fortunately, one of the church brothers arrived and immediately asked the man next door for his burlap sacks, which we filled with shoes. Our employee rolled up all the leather skins, tied them with a rope, and placed them on his back. Meanwhile thousands of people—men, women, and children, most of them Jews from the poorer parts of the city—were moving en masse toward the sea, crying aloud and showing a rising panic. Loaded as we were, we closed the shop and tried to determine our route. We couldn't go home because all the streets were clogged with the thousands running in the opposite direction. Finally, someone suggested the American Evangelical Mission in the western part of the city, where a church friend, a Bulgarian, lived. It's impossible to describe what was happening. The roar of the fire, combined with the cries of the crowds, the howl of the wind, and the falling dark brought to mind Dante's Inferno. It was 10 o'clock when we reached the Mission and were allowed to deposit our packets and bags in the friend's yard. We persuaded Father that we should return once more to salvage what more we could from the store. We now saw the thousands of foreign troops, from the colonies, robbing every shop before them. It seemed to me that only the British were not involved in the looting. By the time we finished, the fire was on the other side of Egnatia. It was midnight when we reached home, in a roundabout way, having climbed first to the upper walls of the city. All of us went to the balcony to view a sight of horror. An ocean of fire was extending from St. Demetrius street to the White Tower and the Gulf of Therma. Flaming timbers exploded toward the sky and were pushed by the strong wind toward other parts of the city. We stayed awake all night. In the morning we three rushed to the shop to find it had burnt. At the Mission, the place was spared together with half of our store's possessions. We thanked God that we had saved that much and our home escaped the fire.

The destruction was unbelievable. Here I must praise the British, who came to the rescue of the homeless and hungry people by making tents and soup kitchens available. I must say that the British of that time behaved with philanthropy and earned the love and appreciation of the people of Thessaloniki and of Makedonia. The French, on the other hand, behaved abominably, following the example of the atrocious General Maurice-Paul-Emmanuel Sarrail, who had refused to allow the water to be used to douse the fire. He had responded to the Greek committee sent for that purpose thus: "Let the city burn to nothing so that the Germans will find it destroyed when they come." This hater of the Greeks was the leading military officer of the Allied powers in Makedonia.

After the fire and its long aftermath, a British naval officer visited the Presbyterian church to ask if any of the "brothers" had lost their livelihood because of the fire. The pastor brought him to our grandfather, who said he didn't need help but thanked him for his care. As the officer was leaving, he greeted each child; when he shook hands with Vassili, the young boy blurted out the only words he knew: "Good night."

Then Officer Thomas Worrell asked: "Do you want to learn English?"

Grandfather, who had pulled the young boy out of school so unjustly, now said, "Yes, this is his desire."

From that day on, until he was reassigned seven months later, this exceptional naval officer climbed the long hill from the port to our grandfather's home to give lessons to the young boy who hungered for knowledge. He left an indelible impression of Christian compassion and grace on my father and a sense of gratitude that I still share.

Many of these tales we learned around our dinner table together with European and Greek history from a man who had a prodigious memory and a gift for telling stories. Only later, when I left home, when I became a mother, did I also feel the emotion that surrounded these quaint accounts of a life.

Who Is My Enemy?

> You have heard that it was said,
> "You shall love your neighbor and hate your enemy." But
> I say to you, Love your enemies and pray for those who
> persecute you.
>
> — Matthew 5:43–44

Years later, steeped in biblical criticism and the understanding that we are all God's children, no matter what name we ascribe to the Divine, I would remember my father's extreme distrust of Turks, Albanians, Bulgarians, and others. "Babá," I asked him once, knowing that it was an unfair question, since the family had known hardships under Turks and Bulgarians, something I had been spared, "do you believe that Christ cares for the Turks also?"

We had been discussing the meaning of the word *echthrós*, enemy, and the meaning of Jesus' words "But I say to you, 'Love your enemies; do good to those who seek to do you harm.'" In response, my father told me again a story I had loved as a child.

It was 1912 and Adrianople was a city besieged in what came to be known as the First Balkan War. Turks on one side, Bulgarians on the other were fighting each other, with the Greek families, unarmed, in the middle, hidden inside their homes, within the suffering city. During those terrible Balkan wars, a temporary victory would bounce from one side to the other. My father remembered the intense hunger of the family, his mother's despair when her children cried out for food. And then came the day when the Ottomans were defeated, and the Bulgarians entered the city victorious. There was never any affection between Greeks and Bulgarians, their enmity centuries old. When we were growing up, the worst thing you could call a fellow Greek was *you Turk*, or *you Bulgar*. That's how intense the ancient and recent memories remained.

The victors needed lodging for their troops and, as usual, the officers had first choice. One of the nicest Greek-owned homes of Adrianople belonged to my grandparents and officers were quartered there. Grandfather spoke fluent Bulgarian and Grandmother was a superb cook. Officers and soldiers used to Protestant worship longed to spend their free time with this hospitable Greek family who shared their faith tradition. My father remembered vivid details from those visits, even the peculiar ones that stay with a child—that the soldiers liked Grandmother's beets and her cherry preserves above all else and couldn't wait to share them with their families back home.

But the memory that affected me in his telling and would stay with me forever after had to do with a different kind of food. The family had the habit of nightly prayers. They read from the scriptures and then knelt to pray. The Bulgarian Christians joined them eagerly, but something strange happened: they wept whenever they prayed. All those age-long enemies, hardened soldiers, wept like little children as they prayed with Greeks. These were tears of joy, Daddy said. As he told us the story, his voice was filled with wonder at the sight he had witnessed in childhood. And I too saw the upturned faces, the tears streaming down the ruddy cheeks, as I envisioned them during our war-darkened nights of Thessaloniki. And those tears entered my young mind and redeemed for me the Bulgarian barbarism I had heard about and was still hearing since they occupied all the Greek land east of us.

Later, as we continued the conversation on "Who is my enemy?" I remembered a certain Sunday in the time of occupation when two German soldiers came to worship with us. To a child of five they looked old, like Daddy, but very different from the green-clad rulers of our universe we saw striding our streets. Josiah and Siegfried entered our *ekklesia* quietly, hats in hand, and sat on the edge of the men's wing. My father could communicate in English, his older brother in French, but I don't think the two Germans had but a few English words between them. How *did* they communicate? Somehow it became clear that they were evangelicals and longed to worship in a familiar environment.

So they sat through long sermons they didn't understand but sang the hymns they recognized. What words did they offer when we all bent our heads for the long prayers uttered from the pulpit? I longed to ask them, but I couldn't. Did they pray for victory, while we, in the privacy of our homes, prayed for their defeat?

My mother, always hospitable, invited them to Sunday dinner. Young as I was, I found it painful to watch how difficult it was to communicate with them. Josiah was blond with pink cheeks and a diffident smile. Siegfried was dark, but his features are a blur in my memory. I can still hear Josiah's plaintive voice as he called my little sister to come closer. *"Komm Eunica, komm,"* is the pleading sound in my head. I never asked if I remembered it correctly. Our baby's name was Evniki, in Greek. "She must remind him of his daughter," Daddy said to our mother, who was so sad for them. But our Evniki was coy and refused to approach them. I stood close to them, filled with curiosity, eager to help Daddy communicate. They showed us pictures of their families, but we didn't know how to respond. My brother made a silly comment about Siegfried's wife's appearance and Dad reprimanded him severely. I do remember that. I think they enjoyed the meal because they came back. But what did the neighbors think? Dad never told us.

"Daddy, are they our enemies? Josiah and Siegfried? They are German soldiers; why are they welcome in our home?"

"Not every German agrees with Hitler," Daddy explained. "And these two men—they are our brothers in Christ. Their nation is cruel, but these two are not our enemies." And that seemed to explain it all. We understood the phrase, "our brothers, our sisters in Christ," but we never questioned why they were the only ones. We simply knew that because they worshipped as we did, they were kin to us.

Finally, what Dad and I disagreed about in my older years was my conviction that all people who sought God were welcome, no matter their religion, and that we all shared this kinship. Dad believed that our kinship was with "the redeemed." Yet, I am convinced as I write this in 2019 that he would be bitterly disappointed in those American evangelicals who equate their faith to their civil religion while ignoring the gospel.

Learning to Dance

But the women of Souli cannot live without liberty.

—Greek folk song

Perhaps if I had stayed in Greece I would have more vivid memories of my primary school years. Those six years blur together and only a few clusters emerge from the fluid passage called Time: my fifth grade, constantly interrupted, because my sister Niki, who had entered first grade, wept so bitterly, so unstoppably, every day, that the teacher, hopeless and irritated, would send for me to walk the little one back home. The school was only a few blocks from our house, and at eight years of age I had to be mother and mentor to a five-year-old. She cried because she was afraid that if she left home our sick mother would die. It was years later that she confessed that fear, but we all suspected it at the time. I think that was the year the civil war was raging, food was scarce, and some boxes from America arrived at the school. I remember the smell and taste of strawberry preserves. And our male teacher, who seemed to be always hungry, was hired by my father to tutor my little sister, who after a while refused to return to school. Under her soft, tender, and adorable exterior, she hid an iron will. During the despair of occupation and the fears of civil war, it is a wonder that so many of us eventually excelled in our studies.

A happier memory is the first chance to dance Greek folk dances. We Protestants were forbidden from any kind of ballroom dancing, but the Greek dances were allowed. So I was mercifully able to participate in an activity I loved. We danced in a circle and we sang:

"As the fish cannot live on land,
neither the flower bloom in the desert,
so the Souliote women cannot live without freedom.
Goodbye to the fountains . . .
goodbye to the mountains and hills . . .
and to you, young women of Souli . . ."

We danced the *syrtaki* or the *kalamatiano,* the leader of the circle holding a large kerchief that she twirled with grace. Who were these women of Souli? The teachers may have thought that this was such an old story that its meaning would not hurt us much, told as it was in a matter-of-fact voice, the one reserved for the serious subject of history. But it is impossible for a Greek voice to remain apathetic; there is something about the culture that pulsates in the voice, that allows pathos to emerge, to color the inflection, to betray the tragedy hidden in the storytelling.

It was during the years of the War of Independence (and the child's mind immediately saw the date: 1821), the liberation from the Turks who had occupied us for four hundred years: so the story always began. The place was Epiros, the western mountainous region of Greece (and immediately my young brain would register: this is where Mammá was born) and the fearful Ali Pasha controlled the region. Souli was one of the many mountain villages of the region. The Souliotes were fiercely independent, and Ottoman leaders had tried in vain to subdue them, even before the war had started. One year, because of treachery, the whole village was empty of men—they had gone away to fight the Turkish army. Twenty-two women and their children, left undefended, feared eventual rape and killing by the Turks. So they danced to their death, jumping from one of the many sharp-edged precipices that guard the startling gorges of Epiros. "Goodbye water fountains, goodbye, goodbye." It was myth or it was history; it was a long time ago, so we could sing and dance the words without feeling the terror and the sorrow. But such stories are absorbed and they embed themselves in the consciousness, never to be ignored. "We Greeks cannot live without liberty. It's better to die than to fall into the hands of Turks." With such stories culture is created, born of myth, legend, and history. To hear the word "Turk" after that early dancing would bring the memory of that deep sadness, the image of women hugging their babies and throwing themselves down the mountains to escape; their fear of falling into the hands of evil men, of enemies. The age-long terror of rape in war is never absent from the fate of women.

The next memory makes me smile with embarrassment. I am now in my last two years of primary school, and I have become somewhat popular with the smart girls, perhaps because of my storytelling. I have started writing a novel with the disciple John as protagonist. A small group of girls follows me home every day to hear the next chapter, which I tell or read as we walk uphill. I am glad I don't remember any of it. My novel must have been influenced by *The Robe*, the popular novel of Lloyd C. Douglas set in the first century, a book I devoured. I never finished writing about John, of course. I must have realized that I could not write anything without *being there*.

However, I was already reading voraciously—any book that I managed to borrow. There was a magazine that arrived at the neighborhood kiosks every week, an encyclopedia for children. My acquaintance with the great classics started with those serialized novels:

Les Miserables, Great Expectations, even some of Tolstoy and Dostoevsky. I read for the story, but the language entered my eyes and my ears and my skin and became a living thing that pulsed and breathed within me. I read to escape because I knew without ever acknowledging it that my mother would never again get well. I read because war was an everyday reality, even though the hated Nazis had left the ravaged land. I read.

Dodona, in the northwestern region called Epiros, was the most ancient of oracles, mentioned by Homer. A mystical, thin place. Author's photograph.

Stairwells

A bad neighbor is a misfortune,
as much as a good one is a blessing.

— Hesiod

Every day of my childhood I ran up and down the two flights of terrazzo stairs in our apartment building. I pause now to contemplate the word "flights." Yes, I flew up and down the steps. I was the one who ran downstairs when Pappous came to see us on his weekly rounds to his sons' homes. From the top of old Thessaloniki, from that cobblestoned neighborhood near the walls of the city he walked, down to the newer city, to visit his daughters-in-law in their own homes: Faithful, good grandfather, *pater familias* of a remarkable clan in that old beautiful city with its tortured history. I saw him approach as I looked down from the balcony, my escape into daydreams. He leaned lightly on his walking stick, and I heard its tock-tock on the pavement. I ran through the apartment and down the steps before he had begun to climb. I bent, took his thin hand and kissed it; then, after releasing it, I felt it placed as a blessing, gently on my head. "Katinoula, Katinoula," he said, his favorite name for me. We didn't speak again. Holding on, we climbed the steps together.

What did my mother and he talk about on those visits as he sipped at the foaming coffee? Was she uncomfortable in his presence as I was years later, alone with my own father-in-law? She never said, and I have no recollection. But our meeting at the bottom of the two flights is vivid, and the memory of his hand on my head a continued blessing.

Around two o'clock Daddy would come home for our midday meal. I would wait on the balcony, looking for him, tired and hot as he was from the climb of the hilly streets while carrying that familiar shopping bag, woven like a fisherman's net, in his hand. Again, I would be the one to run downstairs, to kiss his cheek, to lift the bag filled with fruit, to take his other hand and walk with him up the steps. And Daddy would smile his fondness and his love and all of us would feel the lift of his presence when he entered the apartment. He drank the ouzo cold from the icebox. Always one jigger full, never more, followed by a glass of ice water. And the anise would reach us with its cool aroma while Mother sliced the green cucumbers he had bought on his way home, a smell of dewy freshness. Now secure in Daddy's ritual and discipline, one of us would bring him his bedroom slippers and soon the meal, tasting of summer, would be spread. We ate together, told stories, and laughed.

Those years of running up and down stairs were filled with cousins, friends, and singing. We announced ourselves by whistling four notes recognizable by all the clan—do, lower mi, upper la, sol—and the door would open before we reached the top of the flight. Or someone would whistle from the street and whoever was closest to the window would call out, "Come on up." We gathered around the piano trying out the new songs. Our choir, formed in our home those early years, introduced the Protestant Christmas carols to an Orthodox world not yet jaded by their repetition and commercial misuses. We visited one another's apartment buildings those Christmases and, standing at the bottom of the stairwell, we sang. When we stopped climbing stairs and started punching intercom and elevator buttons, some of that camaraderie deserted us.

On those stairs I met our neighbors. On our landing lived the strange man who, as he reached the top steps, would call out, "Mouse!" his nickname for the daughter who was gawky and had a deformed upper lip, the one who left with her shy American mother to escape the war years. He did not leave with them but another young woman took the place of Mouse, her hair like a huge hat, red and curly around her face. He called her his niece, but for some reason our parents smiled when they heard the word. She played beautiful Chopin nocturnes, and I would lean on the wall to hear each note. Chopin still brings back the memory of that niece who disappeared when the war ended and mother and daughter returned from America. I missed Chopin. But then the serious, kind daughter brought out a record player and the voice of a rich baritone filled the place. She told us that his name was Bing Crosby and looked surprised when we revealed that we had never heard of him.

Directly below us were three Armenian spinsters, the oldest one bossy and mean; the second definitely strange, with hair and eyes always wild, murmuring on the steps; the third like a painted, artificial flower who walked with a limp. We could hear the oldest one beating the mad sister and we would cringe. A man with a gruff voice lived with them. He smelled of cigarettes and spirits when I met him on the steps, and it was he who filled the jugs I took to his corner shop when we had run out of vinegar or wine. I never knew which of the three sisters claimed him. German soldiers came and went—the superior race not despising the poor Armenian women for some strange reason that I learned only as a grown woman.

On the ground floor lived a sad-faced widow, always dressed in black. There was a married daughter with her, but it was the younger one who was the talk of the neighborhood. She was lovely to look at, but her walk was like a peculiar dance, an irresistible motion for children to imitate. We probably would have been more cruel had not the mother looked so sad. One summer day we saw this daughter at the beach having an ice cream with one of the most famous crooners of the fifties. Something about her was both fascinating and alien to us children because we didn't know anything about call girls. The need for survival caused people to do strange thing

An ordinary apartment building with four flights of stairs, two of which I knew with the intimacy of daily encounter: I looked, I heard, I absorbed with all my senses as I ran up and down those terrazzo steps. And down the years I hear again those four notes, do, mi, la, sol, and they fill me with anticipation and then with aching longing as I listen for the echo of that thrilling harmony of our choir resounding through the stairwell at Christmas time, "It came upon a midnight clear that glorious song of old."

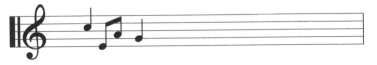

Our clan's musical password.

Holidays and Pastimes

Ayios Vassilis is coming from Caesarea
You are the lady of the manor, Kyria. . .

—the first lines of the New Year's *kalanda*

—Author's Translation

Sugar was scarce, the white version nonexistent for several years. There was something we called "black sugar," which resembled a rough version of the natural or brown sugar of today, but cooks didn't like it. Sweets were so rare that when something layered and honeyed, filled with nuts, appeared, it made the holidays wondrous, delicious occasions.

Our clan celebrated birthdays with great joy. The rest of Greece observed name days, after the saint of the day. Almost every day in Greece has a saint designated to it, so no day feels unblessed. But we weird Protestants honored our own birthdays since, according to St. Paul, we were all saints. Having sugar for some of those occasions made them memorable.

All the women in the family were excellent cooks. Our grandmother was the best, followed by my mother and then two of the aunts. It was a given that those whose origins were in famed Constantinople were the best cooks. My mother was an exception, since she came from the western part of Greece. But she was a quick learner, benefitting from the months she lived near my grandmother, and she excelled in everything that had to do with home and family.

One of the customs that was obviously Oriental was a sweet greeting when a guest first arrived. I remember offering it only to women, not to men. Preserving fruit was an ancient practice that found form as a welcoming gesture in the famous spoon sweets of the region. Whenever an aunt or another woman guest arrived, Mother would lead her to a chair and then she too would sit nearby, ready to chat. That was my cue. From the buffet I removed the small silver tray, a small crystal plate, a silver spoon, and a crystal glass. In the kitchen now, I opened the jar of preserves—figs, orange peel, quince, and bitter orange were favorites. I placed enough of the fruit to fill the silver spoon that rested on the plate. The tray was covered with a pretty embroidered cloth. On it I arranged the crystal plate, now colorful with the preserve, and the cold glass of water, and with care and pride I brought it back to the living room as an offering to the guest. She would eat the sweet; then, holding and raising the glass, she would offer a special wish for the household before drinking the water. *"Stin iyia sas."* To your health. It was Grandmother who made the preserves. She visited the homes of her daughters-in-law in order to do so. One of my fond memories is of her standing at the small gas cooker, stirring the syrup and skimming the top with great patience and without hurry.

Desserts after meals were unknown; only fresh fruit finished our lunch and supper. The birthday treats were *baklava, kadaifi,* or *saragli.* They all reminded us of the east and, very reluctantly, of the Turks, to whom we were never willing to give credit. The phyllo (the word literally means "leaf") for baklava we bought in great, round, paper-thin sheets of dough from a neighborhood store that specialized in this difficult process. The shop was on St. Demetrius Street, parallel to ours, and since I didn't have to cross any dangerous intersections, I was allowed to go shopping for it, drachmas in hand. I remember entering that small store, feeling important, and asking for the phyllo by the weight. There was a very large round table in the middle of the shop, dominating the space, dusted with flour and covered with countless sheets of the delicate dough. The baker would roll them in white paper and weigh them, and then I would emerge from the shop holding one long tube, eager to rush home so mother could layer it into baklava. The preparation was a family affair. We children cracked the walnuts, careful to scoop out all the nut flesh so nothing would go to waste. Then we dropped them in the wooden pestle to pulverize them with the mortar. We did the same with the cinnamon sticks—pound, pound, pound, and breathe in the lovely aroma. Then came the turn of the cloves. Mixed with sugar, the spices were exotic and filled with promise. Layers of buttered phyllo, sprinkled with the nut and spice mixture, were spread inside very wide, round baking pans called *tapsi*. Scored into diamond shapes, each adorned with a clove, the pastries were now ready for the oven. In the city, in those lean years nobody had an oven at home. Two of us would carry the large *tapsi* to the public oven, trusting it to the hands of the busy baker who numbered each *tapsi* before sliding it inside the huge hot beehive built into the wall, exactly on the spot that had the right temperature for the pastry. A couple of hours later, with our special number written on a torn piece of paper, we would return to pick up the baked product. Meanwhile Mother would have had the sugar, water, lemon peel, and more spices simmering on the fire. Eventually, the syrup would be poured on the baked baklava. Covered with a clean tea towel and untouched through the night, it would absorb all the flavors, ready the next day for the birthday celebration.

For *kadaifi* the dough was shredded and for *saragli* it was rolled up and then sliced. We served each diamond-shaped or rolled sweet on crystal plates accompanied by a small silver fork. The adults lifted the plate up before taking a bite, while offering the traditional wish to the birthday person. *"Chronia Polla.* May you live a long time," they would intone. "May the Lord bless you and keep you always."

We children were more interested in playing together than in eating. That was the fun that sugar afforded us—something that brought us together in grandfather's beloved house.

▦ ▦ ▦

Christmas was very similar to birthdays for us. In the war years there were no presents but only memories of toys that father bought from the man whose shop was next door to his own business. He was a very attractive gentleman whose store was mythical, filled with German-made toys. It was a very sad day for us when the war came and it closed. The only Christmas presents I remember getting and cherishing were a tiny porcelain tea set and a book filled with color and pictures, a story about someone named Tom Sawyer. But that was after the war.

The few Christmas trees that adorned the holiday were small and scrawny with real candles clamped on the skinny branches. We decorated them only on Christmas Eve, never earlier. We lit the candles that night while Daddy watched very carefully that nothing else burned. The ornaments were so beautiful—elegant glass balls, masterfully spun and colored. Even today the sight of an old-fashioned Christmas ornament fills me with acute nostalgia.

New Year's Eve was the dearest of the holidays. Little boys in their short pants, their heads shaved and their knees blistered by the cold,

climbed the apartment stairwells to bring the news to the disheart-
ened residents. The boys' jackets were threadbare, patched here and
there, and their cold, ungloved hands held the iron triangle, which
they struck and rang as they sang: "St. Basil is coming from Caesarea;
you are the lady of the house, the lady of the mansion." I noticed only
their pitifully chapped hands and felt sad for them. They were bringing us the *kalanda*, hoping for a few drachmas or for something sweet
to eat, not knowing that there were more fortunate children in other
lands who had sung their Christmas carols the week before dressed in
warm, lovely sweaters and coats.

Mother spent the day baking. We tried to stay up until midnight,
but we never succeeded, so nobody could disprove that St. Basil came
to visit. Before bedtime, we would surround the table to admire the
vasilopita, the large, round cake-bread, a specialty reserved for New
Year's Eve. As Daddy scored the bread into wedges, he would name
every member of the household. We were eager to lift our piece to see
if the hidden gold coin was ours for the year. Even though we were
forbidden from taking superstitions seriously, we knew that the coin
meant good luck. We would taste the *vasilopita* that night, but the
bread would last through the week as a delicious breakfast treat. St.
Basil was expected to arrive that night, bringing presents, as the old
year yielded to the new. But in the war years we learned to be realists,
so we knew presents would not arrive in our home. Still, he was a
good saint, and even an orange was a gift.

Ayios Vassilis (St. Basil) came to be pictured like the Santa Claus or
St. Nickolas of our northern neighbors, but he had been a real person,
a rich Greek bishop of the fourth century, from Cappadocia. He was a
serious theologian and a defender of the faith against heresies, but in
the Greek folklore he is known only as a kindly old priest who arrives
holding an icon, a parchment, and a bamboo stylus. In the *kalanda,*

the folk carols sung especially on New Year's Day, he is invited to sit down and eat with the family, and in one of the stanzas he is called a baker, a kneader of dough. Strange images, unrelated one to the other, appear in these genuine folk songs with hints of historical or legendary reality. Tradition tells us that when the day of taxation arrived in his hometown, the people begged for his help, for they had no money. On a particular day, they were ordered by the governor to bring their jewels and priceless possessions to offer as taxes. So they begged their bishop, Ayios Vassilis, to help save their property—and he did. The treasures, gathered in a heap, were saved, but now came the nearly impossible task of restoring each piece to its rightful owner. How could it be done justly? Ayios Vassilis came up with the solution. Each family was to bake a bread (cake) and hide inside it one of the jewels. All the breads were distributed and, miraculously, each family received the treasures that had originally been theirs. So in this legend lies the tradition of the *vasilopita*, that round, golden-red cake-bread adorned with almond halves and hiding a secret.

⸎ ⸎ ⸎

Children are easily entertained as long as they have friends around, but as we grew into our preteens and teens we needed more than games. In the late afternoon, when the sun no longer baked the balcony and a breeze started to bless us, we sat there embroidering. No matter how intellectual our pursuits, we had to learn what it was that would make a girl a future bride and a wife. We embroidered many doilies and tablecloths, full of colorful birds and flowers, all in tiny cross stitch; when our mothers were girls they had embroidered even their sheets and pillowcases. All of that would eventually become our *prika*, the dowry we brought with us to marriage. I considered it a silly fantasy and it remained so for me. Some of us learned to knit and found relaxation in the activity. And while our hands worked, we gossiped, watched the passersby, and laughed. The boys, chief among them my brother, played soccer in the street and created whatever mischief could escape their parents' notice. For those of us who loved words more than handiwork, the greatest escape was the creation of a new literature for the Protestant community. The best gift of my early teens was writing plays and stories, most of them for performance at our little *ekklesia*. But the chief pleasure was singing, always singing.

*The last formal family portrait with our mother, who shows
the ravages of illness on her once-lively face.*

The Last Long Summer

You milked the light of the universe with your eyes.

—Yannis Ritsos, *Epitaphios*

The ground is dry and the earth parched after months of no rain. The air smells of dry thyme and crushed oregano and, somewhere in the near distance, of animal droppings. Crouched down and giggling, we are following footprints in the dust—all of us cousins, who for the first time are spending the summer in the same village. It is the last long summer, the final summer of my childhood. The village is called Oreókastro, Beautiful Castle, but there is nothing particularly beautiful about it after the devastation of the occupation and the ongoing civil war. We do not find the castle.

The footprints are large—a man's, we determine in our detective fashion—but there are also drops of blood on the very light soil and this is what gives us the frisson of excitement and fear. The oldest two among us are fifteen and the rest of us move down the scale to six or seven. There is no one else nearby, just the dozen of us. It's hot and insects buzz all around—a perfect Greek summer. The earth makes us dizzy with its pungent odors, and mystery adds the sharp tone of fear. After tracking for a while and exclaiming in loud whispers—"It must be a wounded *andartes*, we better be careful!"—we give up and stop. We are not allowed to move too far from the village. We make up stories about this invisible man and snicker, but we know that if he is an *andartes*, a Communist or a nationalist guerrilla, we could be in danger; the civil war is wreaking havoc in some of the villages around Thessaloniki, and the oldest children are cautious. After living through two wars already, even children under ten can smell danger. "We better not go any further. Our mothers will be upset."

The cousins of the other four families had mothers waiting for them. We did not. Our grandparents were in the house we were renting at the end of the one main throughway of the village. The cousins lived closer to the center. All the streets were unpaved. The few inhabitants of Oreókastro had been settled there in 1923, having arrived after the Great Catastrophe, the forced expulsion of Greeks from Turkey. They brought with them the memory of their Pontian village by the Black Sea—Oreókastro—and gave its name to their new home, even though there was no castle nearby. In this tiny village, just a few miles north of Thessaloniki, we city children were in another world. Our rental was a flat-roof structure shaped like an L. We had the long line of the L and a group of three adult siblings had the shorter one. Their family was incomplete like ours—two adult, unmarried sisters, and their younger brother, just twenty years old. He was very attractive, but there was a mystery about him that made his smile look sad. He and I would go into the back yard to collect freshly laid eggs and, watching the flapping of the scrawny chickens together, we would laugh at them. Little by little the secret was shared by the sisters to my grandmother. Their beloved brother was sick with tuberculosis. I immediately felt a kinship to him. Our own mother was in another village, on a higher plateau where the air was cleaner for tubercular patients. We became friends and made a date that we would meet again when I turned twenty. "At the square near your house," he said, "on your twentieth birthday." And he smiled that sad smile of his. "I won't forget," I said, as hope was overshadowed by a dark premonition. I watched him as he washed his face and shaved at the outside sink. It was my first awareness of maleness, of otherness.

We were rather wild that summer, with no one to supervise us. Grandmother must have been very tired cooking for four children, and Grandfather worried more about her than about us. So we saw them only during meals. Our oldest sibling was almost sixteen, and there was already too much weight on her narrow shoulders. Nothing serious was required of my brother—he was the boy, after all—and my responsibility was to look after little Niki. We stayed outside most of the day. Plumbing was at a minimum. There was an outhouse downhill from the living quarters, and to get there we ran by the pigpen. One day we watched in horror and fascination as the sow birthed one piglet after another—a profound shock to city children.

Across from us was a large, unfinished brick home. There were so many unfinished houses those years that the apparent emptiness did not surprise us. Its windows were gaping open—no glass, no shutters. It did surprise us, though, that anyone could live in it. Yet, two older girls, pretty and stylish, were renting it for the summer; perhaps there was a mother with them, but I can't recall a face. The girls made friends with our Doritsa, and in the twilight we, the younger ones, sat nearby and listened to their grown-up talk. I remember once they complained that there was no butter to be had. "How can we eat eggs fried in olive oil?" one of them asked, and for years afterward I would not cook eggs in olive oil. One evening that same girl looked at my sleepy self and frowned. "Don't yawn in front of us," she chastised me. "Yawning is catching." I still wonder: Why do I remember such conversations?

During the day we wandered all over the village with no fear that anyone would harm us, except for our own imaginings when we saw blood drops and footsteps.

All the previous summers of Mother's illness we had spent in the mountain village with her, but this was the last summer, and we had to be separated from her. We didn't know it was the last summer; we never talked about it, but we all suspected it. Daddy rarely came to see us because she could never be alone at night.

One morning, near the end of our stay, I was emerging into the dusty street on my way to the one general store to buy something for Grandmother when I saw a woman's shape in the distance. With the sun's light behind her, she looked unsubstantial but familiar as she walked toward me, yet so out of place in this particular context that for a moment I was disoriented. I ran back to the house and cried out, "Mammá is coming!" All four of us ran outside to meet her halfway. How did she manage to find enough breath, to take two buses, to climb the hills, to come to see us? I still tremble at the thought and find myself running out of breath. I remember nothing else about that visit except for her image on that dusty road, carrying a basket for us, walking with difficulty, trying to smile. I still weep when I remember that scene. She couldn't stay the night.

Daddy came the following Sunday to see us for a few hours, to hold a family gathering, but I already knew the results would not be happy.

"As you know, my children, your mother cannot be alone. I have to go to the city to work every day, so I have to leave her. Doritsa has already spent days with her but now she needs to help your grandmother here. Kostakis is a boy and, of course, Niki is the baby." He looks at me; I know what is coming. "Katinoula, could you go spend the days with your mother, my dear *korê*?"

There is a terrible heaviness on my chest. But how can I say no? He gives me directions and the required drachmas. Doritsa packs my small bag. I will catch the bus to the city in the morning, then walk to another bus stop on Aristotelous Street; from there I should find the right bus for Asvestohóri. Eventually this second bus will stop at the foot of the hill, across from the official sanatorium.

After the loneliness of the bus rides, I climb the narrow track that leads to her house and her suffering.

All the other children are having fun together in Oreókastro, but here I am, alone, eleven years old. Yet, I keep telling myself, Mammá is more alone. I pass the thistles that grow on the path and the few pots of geraniums that struggle to survive on the stone steps of the small cottages. I find the house and enter, trying to appear cheerful. It is a small, whitewashed house, a bright place with lots of light. Mother is lying on her bed against the one wall that has no windows in it. She doesn't seem happy to see me, but then she needs every bit of energy just to breathe. The house smells of medicine. Is she angry with me? Most of my childhood I think she is angry with me. I tell her about her other children, especially little Niki, and then she asks me if my periods have started yet. It is the greatest misery of my young life. I tell her yes, and she is even angrier that she cannot help me.

A woman comes during the day to cook and do house-work and Daddy returns in the early evening, loaded with food baskets, as always. I feel even sadder for him. Keeping a helper has been an additional burden to him because no one wants to look after a sick woman. Finally, an older person from the church community, a refugee, arrives like a godsend. I get glimpses of my father's continuing agony and worry, and I can hardly endure it. Many years later, when I too have children, I think about those days with my dying mother and understand her moods and her pain, and all the poisons that seep in the mind when the body is weak and in agony. Sorrow engulfs me.

Even at eleven years of age I know that I am in a village of the dying. In the twilight, the sick people in the various cottages come outside to lie in their chaise longues and visit with members of their families. There is very little conversation.

It took decades for me to guess at what she was feeling those days. Only my own motherhood revealed her pain to me and it was and remains unbearable. She was still so young. Physical pain and weakness were unacceptable to one who had been very active. Breathing alone was a struggle that robbed her of the ability to show tenderness, and tenderness had been forbidden her for such a long time. Missing her baby daughter must have been her greatest suffering.

Tuberculosis had no cure in the forties. Streptomycin had just come on the market and Dad had spent all his savings to have it sent to us from America, but my mother's disease had progressed to such an extent that the medicine made her much, much sicker. What had given us hope was now an additional destroyer. Doctors knew so little about that medicine.

During the day, I stood at the front door looking at the neighborhood; there were no children to play with. A house was being built across the way, and I was watching how the young builder mixed the cement with water and with deft hands spread it on the concrete slabs. He was shirtless and his back glistened brown and strong in the sun. His muscles flexed and I admired their strength as they bent and lifted great weights. Again I was briefly aware of the strangeness of this man, of his maleness and otherness, of the strong body that was so different from the ones lying on chaise longues, no strength in them. And I understood why those ancient Greeks chiseled the marble to look like this man who was strong, whose body was beautiful.

The summer ended and it was time for me to go to Anatolia College, my new school. We did not return to the same city apartment. We stayed at our grandfather's home, in the Upper City, and only my father remained with our mother in our city apartment. I walked several long blocks to meet the bus that took me to the small suburb of Pylea. There, together with other girls, I waited for the school bus, a converted military vehicle, to take us up the hill. In the afternoon, I returned home carrying my satchel and my worries.

> But where is home? Should I go visit my mother, who is terribly sick, or should I go straight to Grandfather's house further up the hill? This one afternoon, a month after I had begun school, in a still-hot October, I feel an additional urgency to visit my mother. Heavyhearted, I climb the two flights of

stairs. I am stunned to find a lot of people inside.
Why? I see my eldest aunt, Korinna, and I am frightened, because she has not entered our place since my
mother's illness began. I open the door to the bedroom
and I see men surrounding my mother's bed. I see my
father among his brothers and the familiar doctor. Suddenly, my mother lifts her body, sits up, struggling for
breath. She looks so young with her hair loose. She tries
to say something, I call her name, she looks toward me,
and then I run out of the room. Theia Korinna opens
her arms to me and says, "I know it's very hard. But your
father is so good. He will be both father and mother to
you," and only then it hits me. "Is she dying then?" I
cry out and everything else is clouded by the immense
sorrow of the moment and the scream that echoes in
my mind: Is she dying?

Of course we had known it but had never acknowledged it, never had named the horror of our mother's
dying. Now it has been named. Now it is real. And nothing else in the world matters. A while later my father
walks my brother and me to the corner of the street. I
hold his right hand and when he stops to tell us goodbye
I cry out, "You have been so good all these years. Why
doesn't God love you?" He tries to defend his God, but
his face wears the mask of tragedy. On our way to our
temporary home, Kostakis and I cannot speak.

Our mother died that night. Her last words to her husband were:
"Vassili, why are my children so sad?"

The Days After

> The birdcage is left without a bird
> With no water the cistern . . .
>
> —Yannis Ritsos, *Epitaphios*

That night—that lonely sad night when the world stopped for us—crawled by as the time that had no end. We felt utterly lost. We had managed to comfort our youngest—she was just eight years old and fragile—and to put her to sleep on a cot next to ours. Her silent, huge tears reminded us of our mother's desperate weeping. We were occupying the front room left of the large *sala* in our grandfather's home. Doritsa and I lay in the same bed and wept. We tried to speak but we couldn't.

We were all hanging out of the window the next morning, waiting, when the gate to the garden squeaked open and our sad father entered, a wide strip of mourning ribbon encircling his coat sleeve. "Ach," I cried, "we'll never hear her voice again." My cry has echoed down the decades.

Whose idea was it that we children should not attend the funeral? We never really found out. The burial was the day after the death. One of the old-fashioned black carriages with the plumed black horses came to take her away; we learned all this from our oldest cousin who lived on the same street and who was allowed to attend the final event. Everyone in attendance followed on foot behind the hearse. It moved slowly up the hill to the Upper City, where the cemetery of the Protestant Christians was located. The Brits had used that land to bury their own dead starting with World War I, and our congregation now claimed the site. My cousin described what happened after the service and the burial. A great desperate cry arose from the throat of our father, who, calling her name, fell on top of the grave. That is what my cousin told us, and that is what stayed with us. Everything else was kept from us.

That evening our father came to see us, to be with us for a few hours, and all I could do that day was to hold on to the back edge of his jacket. He remembered later that we were trying to comfort ourselves by learning a hymn that spoke of joy. We were children, after all, unaware of irony. Daddy's sorrow and aloneness were so profound that no effort on our behalf could diminish them. He was pitiable, but so were we. I marveled in bitterness for days that the sun rose, that the family dressed as usual, that our aunt and grandmother prepared food for us to eat.

Days later, after the apartment had been cleaned and painted, we returned to Number 9, Stratigou Doumbioti Street. The little one acted as if something alien and frightening was present, and Daddy took her for a long walk while we prepared the rooms. At what point during that week I was called to my grandparents' room in the house up in the Old City I don't remember. But my quiet grandfather opened his Bible and read to me from First Thessalonians. It was a letter written by St. Paul to the first Christians in our city; we of Thessaloniki knew that. Some lazy translator had failed to write Thessalonikians, and the English has retained the wrong spelling—Thessalonians. "The trumpet shall sound and the dead shall be raised incorruptible," Pappous read to me with the utter conviction of one who harbored not the slightest doubt that it would be so. And I believed him and St. Paul on that day and held on to the promise as the drowning person holds on to the life raft. It was exactly what I needed at that time.

The weeks that followed are best lost in Lethe, the river of forgetfulness in ancient Greek mythology. The first days after the death of a loved one are so grim, so filled with grief that it is impossible for anyone else to enter into that sorrow. Our father asked us to write about our mother, but it was too soon; we were still raw and we could not do it. Later, when writing became my lifeline, I could not write anything without writing about her also. Years later I read the heartbreaking letters our father wrote to her every day after her death; unbeknown to us he visited her grave, where he wept uncontrollably. Doritsa, being the oldest, wore black for a year, something I knew my mother would not have approved. I remembered clearly how she had spoken against obvious demonstrations of grief.

Eventually, I returned to school feeling different, feeling alone and surprised that life could simply go on. But it did. Miss Mary Ingle, our dean, her blue eyes vivid, hiding what later I knew to be sympathy, said to me: "You must now pay attention to your studies. Your mother would wish for you to do well." I wiped my tears and left for class. I felt like a specimen: "This is the girl who has no mother."

Pretending All Is Well

> Children suffer not (I think) less than their elders
> but differently. . . . Grief in childhood is complicated with
> many other miseries.

> —C. S. Lewis, *Surprised by Joy*

For a while we struggle on our own. An Armenian woman, her bowlegs strong under her short skirts, walks to our place every day to serve as housekeeper. She claims to be one of us—the moral and moralistic evangelicals—but she doesn't act like one. There is something brazen about her but, to our dismay, many years pass before we learn that she encouraged our brother's sexual fantasies to a point where his precarious and fragile emotions turned to depression. At that time, we didn't know what was happening to him—living with a strict father who understood nothing about the teenage years and an unscrupulous young woman who tempted him in the opposite direction from teachings that were impossible to follow. Our brother's serious depression would recur during those awful, lonely years. He would sit on a small dining room chair in an almost fetal position, his head in his hands, unable to move or to go to school.

In the afternoon, the Armenisa, as we call her, reads our coffee cups. We drink our strong Greek coffee, turn the demitasse cup over on its saucer, wait for the thick dregs to slide into creative patterns and then, snickering, we gather around her to hear what she sees in its grooves and paths.

We listen and grin but never believe a word she says. All of us remember our mother's strong admonition: "You will never believe the superstitions of our fellow Greeks. There is no such thing as the evil eye. Only God has power over your lives; no one else does." She had read a book about a young woman's visit to a fortune teller who predicted that on a certain day, soon, she would die. The young woman believed in the prediction, suffered loss of appetite, sank into depression, and died on the appointed day. That story horrified our mother who had not heard of self-fulfilling prophecies. She repeated to us what she had read and then said: "You will never go to a fortune teller. You will never believe in predictions. We are people of the Word of God. We are not allowed to have any idols." It is the only admonition I remember from my mother. It stayed with me, with us all. Unlike our fellow Greeks, we grew up totally free of superstitions. Even in America, when I hear "knock on wood," or "fingers crossed," I cringe. The Armenisa didn't last long. Maybe she too was cursed by the evil eye. She walked away on her high heels never to be missed.

Many years later, on a visit to Crete with my two daughters, I decided to show them Anoyia, the village razed in 1944 by order of the murderous German commander, Muller. The village had been utterly destroyed in an act of retaliation, and the male population shot. Anoyia had been rebuilt; its inhabitants were famous for their striking physical resemblance to the Minoans depicted on the Knossos frescoes. Small boned and delicate, the women still possessed those fine curls one sees on Minos's palace walls. These women, dressed in their perpetual black, excel in weaving rugs in stunning colors. I wanted my young daughters to feel the place. But my Maria, ten years of age and achingly pretty, became sick on the winding mountain road, and by the time we arrived at the village square she could not face the food the villagers had spread before those who had arrived on the bus tour. Ironically, most of the tourists were German. The bus driver reprimanded me severely for not protecting my daughters from the evil eye; I had not pinned on their shirts the blue and white amulet, the *phylaktó*—the glass eye talisman many Greeks wear. I laughed it off. A black-clad Anoyian sitting next to me at the table said, "Come, my *korê*, bring your daughter to my home; there, she can lie down." My other daughter, Niki, decided to stay at the table, absorbing the Greek atmosphere and language.

Grateful and relieved to leave the German tourists behind, I accepted the hospitality of the woman I thought of as the Minoan; we followed her to her sparsely furnished hut. The one-room home, scrupulously clean, contained one narrow cot. She placed a white sheet on it and invited Maria to lie down; then she pulled up a chair for me and one for herself. Unfolding a very large square cloth, like an oversized handkerchief, she tied the ends into knots and started an incantation I could not understand. It was a poem in a Cretan dialect and, mesmerized, I listened. After a while, Maria raised her head to ask me: "Mama, what is she doing?"

I smiled. "I think she is exorcising the evil eye that made you sick."

Maria burst out laughing and the dear woman turned to me: "See, she is better already."

▦ ▦ ▦

Across from us on Stratigou Doumbioti Street, the side-by-side apartment buildings held other temptations and several young men. Lakis was the dangerous one. He was probably eighteen but seemed a grown man to us. He sat on his balcony, his dark mustache making him look much older and, staring at our building, he played the accordion as darkness fell. We thought it such a romantic sound. *"Bésame, bésame mucho,"* and "Don't fence me in"; translated into Greek with other songs of the forties, these were so familiar that we hummed them together with his playing. Our brother was utterly in his grip. Lakis smoked, so Kostakis had to smoke, something fiercely forbidden in our community; this was done secretly, but someone always told on Kostakis and then there were quarrels and recriminations. There was a Clark Gable mystique and swagger about Lakis and we found it impossible not to stare back at him and to wonder who was the object of his songs. Later I found out that he was madly in love with a girl in our building and she returned the passion. Why they didn't marry I don't know, but I suspect that her father, together with all the fathers in the neighborhood, disapproved of him. The last time I saw Lakis he was in my brother's apartment. The romantic young man was bald by then and had a German wife, a comfortable-looking hausfrau. I looked at her and wondered if he ever told her about those war years and their aftermath, about his constant flirting, and his sway over my brother, who now looked at Lakis with something akin to pity.

There were more boys than girls in our neighborhood, and a few lonely women. Our postman would walk long distances carrying his sack. He entered the front door of each building and, standing under the stairwell, he would call out the names on the envelopes. Occasionally, he would disappear in some woman's place for a longer time than was necessary for the delivery of letters. But I remember him with affection. When I returned to the same apartment years later, my young husband in Vietnam, the postman worried about me. He would call my American name with obvious glee when a letter arrived from Vietnam. "You let your best girl get away," he told my older sister. Even in that large city, there was a human connection I still remember with longing.

My brother's friend Yiorgos climbed the stairs to sit in the kitchen with us, bringing us news of forbidden Hollywood. He told us about a man called Frank Sinatra and about a luscious-looking woman by the name of Ava Gardner. I thought Sinatra was nothing to look at. Yiorgos was amused by our innocence and ignorance; he was already a man of the world, and he tried hard to educate us. He felt sorry for us, but I felt sorry for him because he lived in an apartment below street level. Maybe Hollywood stories comforted him.

Once a week I walked to Aunt Ida's home for a lesson in English. She lived near the Ayia Sophia church, one of the best-known locations in the city. Across from that majestic Byzantine church, at the corner, was the sunken ancient church of John the Baptist. It was a catacomb, but the garden was open for all to see, and I would stop every time I passed to look down from the railing at the fallen marbles and the fountain. We were used, those scant years, to the sight of injured men or gypsy women sitting on the sidewalk, begging. We learned to ignore them, since we had no money to spare. One day, as I crossed the square to approach the sunken church and Aunt Ida's building,

I saw a man sitting by the railing and I knew that I had to walk by him, but that I would not stop to stare at the fountain. It was too late to cross to the other side of the street. He called out something and I saw that he was exposing himself, this pathetic creature, exposing himself to a twelve-year-old. I happened to be wearing a national costume that day because we had had a celebration at school. I had been so proud of my outfit and now I was disgusted. Aunt Ida and her brother were very solicitous when they saw how upset I was but they couldn't adequately answer my question: Why are some men so terribly stupid? I was furious that he had spoiled the pleasure of looking at the catacombs.

Summer of 1950

> If I may trust my own experience, the sight of adult
> misery and adult terror has an effect on children which is
> merely paralyzing and alienating.
>
> —C. S. Lewis, *Surprised by Joy*

I thought we had established a livable routing. Our long-suffering grandparents were living with us once again; Daddy went to work and we went to school; Grandmother cooked and the three older children were navigating the agonies of the teen years with a seriousness that today's teens could not begin to comprehend.

One afternoon I returned from school to find my older sister waiting for me. Four years create a great distance between teenagers, and we seemed to have very little in common. My grandmother stayed in the kitchen, the door closed. Doritsa closed the French doors to the living room and sat next to me:

"Listen," she said, and for some reason I felt a renewed dread. "You know how difficult all this must be for our grandparents. And for Daddy."

I bristled. "We are getting along all right, aren't we?"

"No," she said, and there was sadness in her voice, "we are not. It's not easy for a man to live alone."

"He has *us*," I cried, "and you are talking like *them*."

She ignored me.

"The time has come for us to consider the possibility that Daddy will marry again."

"No," I cried. "I will never agree. Never."

I could see that my sister was very uncomfortable, almost in tears. I was already weeping with fury. We talked on and on, moving from anger to more tears to a near agreement and then to furious resignation. I started bending when Doritsa said: "Think about *me*. I have become a mother too soon. I too would like to enjoy some freedom." And that took away all my anger.

Little by little it emerged that our grandparents approved of the decision. I imagine they were very tired of us and our quarrels. The big question that loomed like a nightmare was *Who will take our mother's place?* We were reassured (by whom? I don't think it was our father, who was embarrassed to talk to us) that he would not make a decision, a choice, without our approval.

And now the whole Greek evangelical world seemed to get involved. Match making must have been going on beneath the surface for the past two years, until one day our father announced that we would be going to Kerkyra, known to the outside world as Corfu. Because of the occupation and the civil war that had just ended, travel had been a luxury we had not enjoyed. The only means of transport remained by sea.

To my surprise and immense gratitude later, I was to accompany my father, together with my younger sister. We were to travel to Kerkyra, where we would meet the woman none of us had seen, the one who had come highly recommended and who had corresponded with our father. It was my first long sea voyage. The vessel held quite a few people, but I preferred staying on deck during the long night. We all seemed shell-shocked after the frightful decade of wars and deprivations. There were many soldiers on board, but I remember little of human beings because the sea and the moon and the silent dark mountains we were gliding by held so much beauty and mystery that it made my heart sing and ache at the same time. I am sure we must have changed ships in Piraeus, but all that has been erased by what was awaiting us.

We saw Kerkyra in the morning light. The sight was so different from that of Thessaloniki that I was breathless and wary. I thought we were entering a foreign land, not a place that was Greek. A rock-like castle rose before us, but all the images blend and shimmer under the Greek sun, overlaid by the extreme anxiety of meeting a strange woman who aspired to be our mother. A huge lump sat on my stomach and would not move. Someone was waiting for us in the noisy port; someone drove us to one of the narrow streets of the main city, but again all the details are lost. I could sense my dad's great apprehension, and I felt my little sister's thin body pressing to my side, trying to hide herself. I remembered again the first year of her schooling—how I was pulled from class again and again because she would not stop weeping, and I had to walk her back home—I, the fourth-grader.

When we entered the home of the prospective bride and her father, we stood apart from the adults, Niki and I, and watched as the woman rushed to our father and kissed him on the lips. I felt Niki freeze next to me, and I tried not to feel, not to think. I noticed the woman was wearing thick glasses, and she was obviously excited and pleased that we were there. Now Niki and I were covered by a dread reminiscent of October 1948, the month of our mother's death. I sensed it in my little sister and saw it in the tears that started their inevitable track down her thin cheeks. Feeling sick, I made an effort to be polite, but words wouldn't come.

That first shock stayed with us through the day. Kerkyra was so beautiful, but our bewilderment and despair colored even that beauty. Later, when we were alone at last, our father, looking miserable, asked us what impression we had of the woman he planned to marry. Young as I was, I sensed that he was looking for an excuse not to go through with it. Niki continued her silent tears with a stubbornness that could not be ignored. "I don't want her," she said, and that was that. I tried to be kinder. "Daddy, I don't think she will fit in with our family. I think it will be a bad mistake."

How embarrassed he was as he disentangled himself, I could only guess. I am sure he used us as his primary excuse. The whole trip had become a fiasco, an utter disaster. The three of us sailed away from the stunning island, saying very little. Little Niki was triumphant; I was very quiet and decided that I would not talk about it to anyone. On the return trip I focused on the beauty of the Greek sea, on the moon's reflection following us throughout the night, and on the dark shapes of the mountains as we glided past them. That melancholic beauty would stay with me, but everything else about the boat journey itself would be forgotten. The reason for our trip to Kerkyra was never mentioned in the presence of my father.

When, decades later, my husband and I were driving on the mainland, very close to the island of Kerkyra, I refused his desire to visit it. Something inside me kept me from returning to that place of emotional distress.

The next year, the passenger trains were running again and I made my first land trip to Athens. Once more, Daddy and little Niki were with me. Whenever the train went through a tunnel, we emerged covered with soot. How I hated that dirt.

We were on our way to our first camping experience, Niki and I. The evangelical community of Greece had been given choice property on the promontory of Sounion and this camping was an experiment, a relief offered to children who had survived a decade of war. Everything was primitive—the tents, the cots, the dining hall, the whole establishment. From the very first I knew we were in trouble. Niki, who had refused to attend first grade, now refused to stay at camp. Her unbearable weeping started again as soon as our father left us, and here I was once more having to suffer her misery, trying to act as the grown-up, with little success. And as before, she got her way and was rescued from the camp.

I was told by my father, in his embarrassed, careful way, to pay attention to a certain woman who was on staff. "See what you think of her." I knew that he must have been talking about another prospective bride, but I refused to play detective, so I came across as arrogant and stuck up, I was told later.

I made one good friend, Sophia, and together we wrote plays and found a crew to perform them with us. This is the best memory of that miserable summer. Afterward, I stayed in Athens for a while, having a taste of what it meant to be poor and a refugee while delighting in the great city that in those days had improbably clean air and light like no other.

A widow, a refugee of the Great Catastrophe of 1922, and her daughter, Rena, lived in the makeshift settlements that sprang in Athens to house many of the displaced Greeks of Turkey. The housing was ramshackle, made of tin and wood; the temporary structures were makeshift shacks with one bedroom per family and a corner for cooking. These two women were extremely hospitable and for the sake of Rena's friendship with my older sister, they asked me to stay with them for a few days. For the first time I experienced something of the lives of refugees, a lesson I would not forget. So I came to know the Athens of the fifties, walking with Rena on its boulevards and side streets, all unclogged by traffic. At fourteen, I was learning to take care of myself. There was poverty even in Athens, a dearth of vehicles and a clarity in the atmosphere—an image that has stayed with me and has made me dislike the modern unbearable traffic and the tourist crowds that pollute the city's monuments. This is the Athens I always long for—the freedom to enter the Parthenon, to wander around the sacred rock without running into anyone else, to walk all over the Acropolis in peace. And later, in the sixties, the still-modest *tavernas* of the Plaka became a pleasure never to be repeated.

The Parthenon as seen from the Propylaea. Author's photograph.

A view from the temple called Theseion. Author's photograph.

A New Mother

Then he said to the disciple, "Here is your mother."
And from that hour, the disciple took her into
his own home.

—John 19:27

Athens, the fabled capital, now came to be of personal, not just historical, significance to our family. Maria's family was as important in the Athenian Protestant circles as ours was in Thessaloniki. The father, John Demopoulos, was one of the founders of the strong evangelical fellowship of the capital, a taciturn man who first started me on the road to intelligent doubt. His wife was a strong woman who dominated the family. There were three daughters and two sons. The sons were very handsome young men, the women not as much. But they were good people. All of the children were unmarried. The youngest of the daughters was engaged to a man who became an important part of our own lives also. Their engagement, in the typical fashion of the lean years, lasted a very long time.

Maria, the oldest of the daughters at thirty-seven, was still single. The boys had to wait until all three elder sisters were married, so they had long-term liaisons, but like the good sons of those times they lived at home, under Mama's thumb. It was the Greek way.

Maria was destined to become our new mother. My father, who met her right before their wedding in brief encounters, fell in love with her and became happy again. We talked among ourselves while the couple were on their honeymoon in Kifissia and decided we would call her *Mammá*—to be kind, to please our father, and to make an effort to become a whole family again. Besides, it was the Greek way. She was a good woman with a big heart and a full, trained, singing voice. From the first afternoon, when I returned home from school to a family that was no longer orphaned, I knew that I would like her. I played the piano while she sang Handel and Grieg. Whenever I hear or sing Handel's "Largo" and Grieg's "Solveig's Song," that first afternoon with a new mother in the home comes back to me with a poignancy that only music can recall. Maria was an excellent cook and was very courageous, something I didn't recognize until later. She entered a close-knit family to live in the same apartment as her predecessor, without complaining, as far as I could see, and taking on four strong-willed, opinionated children.

Laughter returned to our family and our poor grandparents returned to their room in their home up in the Old City.

Niki had someone to care for her again, and we enjoyed Maria's freer spirit, her more enlightened Protestantism. It was her father who first asked me the question that stayed with me and started me on the creative course of doubting and searching for answers. I was talking theology with him, as usual, and he asked me one time: *What if we are wrong?* I was stunned. I had been taught certainty, absolute certainty, and here was this wise man asking this important question. I never forgot it.

While our home life was finding its new pace, I continued to walk several blocks and then ride two different buses to school every day. My name, with its many diminutives, now changed to Katy at school, pronounced *Ketty* by the Greeks. My cousins, to tease me, referred to me as the Americana. I don't think it was complimentary. Daddy continued to call me Katinoula and the aunts Katinitsa. I was developing personalities to fit the names.

Doritsa and I continued to play the pump organ at church and the choir was thriving. As I sat on the bench in front of the instrument, there, on the diagonal, my side vision would catch the arrival of the congregants. One night there was a flash of white as a man's hand stretched to place a Navy hat on the coat rack. We knew everyone who attended our small *ekklesia*. Who was this new person? The hat was that of an officer of the Coast Guard. For several weeks, he entered, worshiped, and disappeared. When eventually we met him, we saw a very handsome face, green eyes with long lashes, wavy black hair, and a chiseled, dimpled square chin. Like most Greeks of the day, he was rather short. Doritsa never flirted, unlike the rest of us. Now she started blushing every time Manolis entered the *ekklesia*. We spent time teasing her, while the women entered into their favorite pastime, matchmaking. How soon Manolis became aware of all the attention aimed at him, I don't know, but their courting must have been excruciating, since there was never any privacy in our clan. Of course, at first they had to give each other their word, as the custom was, in front of the parents. Then came the formal engagement, and later, after I was no longer in Greece, the wedding.

Manolis was from the fabled island of Crete. His father was murdered when the Germans invaded the island in May 1941. In that battle his mother lost a leg and an eye. The fierceness of the Cretan soul was inside the man who became my brother-in-law, whose devotion to my sister was legendary for sixty-three years, and whose two sons grew to be tall and upright, educated Greeks. To my sister Niki and me he became an affectionate and humorous brother, a steady presence in our lives. Above all islands in Greece I love Crete, and my dear brother Manolis was the reason.

Anatolia College

As we face this changing, chaotic, fear-ridden world,
we can take comfort in the great, unchanging truths,
and in the fact that the greatest hope for the future
still lies in the ability of our schools to send out into
the world men and women who will try
to live by these eternal truths.

—Carl Compton in 1959,
in his commencement address
to Grinnell College students

Today, on a hill overlooking Thessaloniki and the Gulf of Therma, an exquisite campus stands unique among the city's schools. It's not surrounded by concrete but by greenery. Its buildings are scattered on two sides of the highway that leads to the village of Panorama, but the modern elegance is a far cry from the school I attended immediately after World War II. Anatolia College even then had a reputation as a fine school, but its history was even more remarkable than its educational quality.

In the early part of the nineteenth century, a great revival swept American Protestantism into the Second Great Awakening. In this spiritual revival the names of colleges that today are among the wealthiest and most respected universities in America feature quite prominently. In our secular times, it is preposterous to contemplate that many of these institutions of higher learning started as religious training grounds for young men and (later) women who, filled with missionary fervor, were eager to evangelize the world. Among the first was a group in Williams College, who were persuaded that they needed to carry the gospel of Jesus Christ to heathen peoples for their personal salvation. As a result, the American Board of Commissioners for Foreign Missions was created, with Boston as its headquarters and with funding from individual churches, mostly Congregationalist, and with no help from the government. What is of concern here because of Anatolia College and my personal family history is the creation of the Western Asia Mission. When the board started sending missionaries to the Ottoman Empire, which, at that time, stretched over enormous territories, they had no idea of the cultures of these lands and of the dizzying complexity of ethnicities and languages within them.

Courageous young people, convinced of their mission and their role as bearers of the Good News of personal salvation, launched themselves under extremely difficult conditions into chiefly Muslim territories whose populations also included Jews, Greek Orthodox, and Armenian Gregorian Orthodox adherents. Mission centers were established from the Black Sea and the Caucasus Mountains in the north and east of the Ottoman Empire to the Arab territories in the south and the Balkans in the west. The Muslims were utterly resistant to being proselytized, while the Greek Orthodox, whose very identity was bound to the continuation of the ancient Byzantine faith they claimed, were equally resistant. But the Armenians eventually proved to be a bit more approachable. Traveling under primitive conditions and meeting profound religious differences bound up in ethnic identities did not deter these intrepid missionaries. Initially bent on offering only theological education, they bided their time by teaching young women about hygiene and crafts, and by preparing a few young men to become pastors.

The hinterlands of the Ottoman Empire consisted of small agricultural villages whose peasant populations lacked the wealth and amenities found in cosmopolitan Constantinople (Istanbul) and in Smyrna (Izmir). Hygiene, medicine, and education were not available in these forgotten areas. Yet, those were the places the missionaries chose for their work. The mission that created Anatolia College in 1886 was located in the Asian, northeastern part of Turkey, in Marsovan (or Merzifon), in a stunning physical location on a large plain at the foot of the snow-capped White Mountains. The Greek word for sunrise and for the east is Anatoli, so the school was called Anatolia. The school song, "Morning Cometh," reflects this concept of sunrise and of the east.

In America, the missionary zeal of New England colleges and churches spread west to found important educational institutions, among them Grinnell, Oberlin, and Carleton Colleges. And even hardier, more dedicated graduates, both men and women, left their comfortable American lives to travel by ship, and then on horseback and on foot, in roundabout ways, to reach and teach at this remote new college in Turkey, seven days' travel from Constantinople. Most of the students were Armenians, young men molded for the ministry; an adjoining school for girls trained young women to be good homemakers, seamstresses, and weavers. Eventually, Greeks from the Pontus region by the Black Sea, attracted by the lure of education, would travel to study at Anatolia also.

Among those who found their way to this educational oasis in the midst of ignorance and poverty was a young athlete from Grinnell, Carl Compton, who was destined to bless both the college and all of Greek Makedonía with his presence and dedicated work. After an initial internship at Anatolia, he returned to Iowa to marry the lovely Ruth McGavren. Their honeymoon trip turned out to be a very long journey of service that brought them to Japan, China, and Siberia, where they spent several months working under the auspices of the YMCA. Their ultimate destination was the Caucasus Mountain region, where they worked with Armenian refugees fleeing persecution. With American pragmatism and organizational skills, they trained weavers to use the abundant wool of the region and to sell its products; Ruth taught little children to read and write and risked her health to serve fearlessly despite life-threatening epidemics. All this happened during the terrible years of World War I. Near the Black Sea they were caught between fighting sides and barely escaped their bullets.

It took a long time for the Comptons to reach Anatolia College at a time when the Turkish state was changing, and a new nationalistic fervor was turning them against the Armenians and Greeks, who for centuries had been their neighbors. The Turks' persecution, and the massacre of both Armenians and Greeks, endangered also the school's population. Members of the faculty and the student body were hanged and the American teachers were ordered to leave Anatolia. But because the school was filled with orphaned children, the Comptons, being the youngest foreigners, were allowed to stay in order to care for them. Dangers, fear of abduction and of death, surrounded them day and night; only their American nationality saved them on several occasions. Yet, even though their safety remained precarious, they did not abandon their charges.

The above is a tiny summary of the courage Carl and Ruth Compton showed early in their married life—in Russia between 1917 and 1919, in the college until 1922, and then in two years of service with the Near East Relief Association. The dangers brought on by extreme nationalism and hostility caused the Board of Missions to close the school and transfer it to Thessaloniki in 1924. Carl and Ruth Compton joined the faculty of this new college in 1925. They had been educating young Greeks for a decade and a half when again war forced the school to close in 1940 and the American faculty to leave the occupied land.

When Carl Compton returned four years later, he found that commerce, industry, transportation, and agriculture had ceased to exist because of the ravages of the Nazi occupation.

During those miserable years of occupation of Greece, Carl Compton was working in Washington for the immediate relief of the suffering population of the country he had come to know before the war. In August 1944, word came that the Germans would be retreating. A British liaison unit would be the first to move into Greece; with them they would bring personnel from the United Nations Relief and Rehabilitation Association (UNRRA), Carl Compton among them. The initials UNRRA became for us a lifeline mantra.

It was November before they were able to land in Greece; Carl Compton was assigned to northern Greece, to Thessaloniki, which he knew well. When the relief team arrived by sea, they were not able to enter the deep and once beautiful harbor because of the ships the Germans had wrecked and sunk into the waters. The city seemed deserted and the once elegant Mediterrané hotel facing the harbor had no water, no heat, and no electricity, but there was nowhere else to stay. The drachma was worthless and the shops were shuttered. Eager to see his college, Carl Compton found that Anatolia now housed the Fourth Indian Division of the British Army. The campus had been nearly destroyed by its former occupants, the Germans, who had even smashed the plumbing before leaving. From October 1940 to the end of the war against the Italian Fascists, Anatolia had housed the wounded Greek soldiers. When the calamity of occupation began in April 1941, the school became the German headquarters for their Balkan operations. When UNRRA arrived, the Brits became the last foreign occupiers.

Carl Compton was appalled at the devastation of northern Greece. Starvation and misery they had expected, but they were shocked to find the hostilities between the nationalists and the Communists still in force. Cries of *Laocratia!* (the power of the common people) surprised them, because all they saw among the *laos*—the people—was a longing for jobs and for peace, not this terrible fratricide. We, the citizens of the city, had become so used to the word *laocratia* that we no longer heard it, because we knew that the people had no power. Most of rural Greece, especially Makedonía, was controlled by the *andartes,* the Communist guerrillas, but they did not interfere with the work of the UNRRA personnel.

A child needs heroes, and the Comptons were mine, though, at that time, I knew nothing of their remarkable history. I rarely saw Dr. Compton, but Mrs. Compton came to our classroom that first year to teach us the American Christmas carols. She was a very beautiful woman, totally unadorned, with her hair white even in her middle years, soft around her face and pinned in a bun on the very top. "Away in a manger," she sang, "no crib for his bed, the little Lord Jesus lay down his sweet head." We repeated each phrase while the melody and the words entered me as a balm at a time when I was raw inside.

I didn't know then that her husband was a true hero. When he returned to Thessaloniki in November 1944 the civil war was still ravaging the countryside. He found the people poor and hungry beyond his imagining, but he struggled through enormous obstacles as the head of UNRRA to bring them some relief. He wrote to his family descriptions of what he saw in our tragic land:

*A terrible nightmare . . . The amount of wartime destruction is
appalling, much of it willful with no military purpose. Every telephone
and telegraph pole is chopped down, bridges destroyed, hundreds of
villages burned. No money to pay labor.*

As he traveled on the pot-holed, unpaved roads of Western
Makedonía, he came close to despair:

*The needs are almost overwhelming—especially for clothing, blankets,
window glass, for material for repair of homes in villages. Business,
industry, and transport are almost nonexistent and thousands walk up
and down with nothing to do . . . .*

His love and appreciation for the people are evident in his letters:

*"It is terrible to have so little to give to people who need so much.
Nobody begs for anything except work. How they continue to be so
cheerful and courageous I just can't see. . . . the country has been
stripped of everything. . . ."*

His beloved Anatolia was unrecognizable. Yet, despite the horrors
Dr. Compton encountered upon his arrival, with the help of UNR-
RA and the determination of the people, the country was on the way
to recovery by the spring of 1945. The best gift of America, ever, was
the Marshall Plan. The school reopened in September of the same
year. Three years later, I arrived as a lonely and hesitant student.

The campus my class entered in 1948 was still in poor condition and classes were held in the old military barracks, now converted into classrooms. It didn't bother us, for we felt privileged to be attending an American school. If any of us had been born in luxury, the ten previous years had erased that memory. From the various points of our city, we arrived at the bus stop in the village of Harilaou to stand waiting for one of the two school buses to pick us up for the short drive to our school. We looked with envy when my classmate Tessa arrived on a jeep. She was the daughter of the publisher of one of the major newspapers of the city. Even a jeep seemed a luxury those days. In our family we considered it the utmost in privilege to ride in our uncle's jeep; he was a major in the army and so he had rights the rest of his brothers lacked.

After we returned to our apartment following our mother's death, our father woke up every morning to prepare my breakfast and lunch. He had many gifts, but cooking was not among them. I came to hate the dried, fried eggs he packaged for me, thoroughly embarrassed to eat them. School lunches were not a habit in the Greek schools of the day, but we were too far away to return home for lunch. Daddy woke me at seven and I felt oppressed that everyone else in the house could sleep longer.

I walked alone to the bus stop, which was several city blocks downhill, at Egnatia Street. The bus drove us east, outside the then-city limits, past some elegant old homes that had belonged to rich Jews, and then past some tobacco factories. Several women climbed down at those stops and I felt sorry for them having to work in a factory. I knew nothing about their lives; everything I felt was a result of conversations I had heard. I didn't know how passionately supportive of labor unions I would become later in my life.

Harilaou was a suburb of Thessaloniki, sparsely occupied, more a village than part of a city, and there the municipal bus left us to await the school bus, which had bare, hard seats. It groaned uphill, and I delighted at the sight of the small fields of wheat waving in the morning breeze, ethereal and golden under the rising sun. One or two houses stay in the memory, but for the most part all that remains is a quick and pleasant drive. When I made the same drive recently, there was not a single signpost reminiscent of that daily, long-ago journey.

I had the reputation of being a good student, but I made very little effort. I loved everything that had to do with words, but I could not be bothered with what didn't come naturally to me. I was ambitious about literature, writing, and music but not particularly eager to excel in other subjects. Though I became popular (something that still remains a mystery), being elected class president without any effort on my part, I felt distant from my surroundings. I was more comfortable observing than participating—except for chorus, theater, and anything related to literature.

Miss Almquist taught us English. We all wanted to be like her. Young and blonde with that exotic upturned nose we Greeks envied, she was our ideal woman. In her midi-length skirts and loafers, she walked with a kind of bounce, her rich loose pageboy accompanying the rhythm with every step. It was a hairdo we had not seen before; shoulder-length, it turned up at the ends. Her full lips were very red with the favorite lipstick color of those days. Several upper-class girls were in love with her. Her secret, knowing smile was irresistible. What I cherish about her memory is that she explained the peculiarities of English grammar in a way that I absorbed immediately and never forgot: That *hair* and *news* take a single verb—such a peculiar construction to a Greek speaker. That one can respond with "It is I," instead of the Greek *Ego Eimai*—I am. Strange to a Greek ear. And the three versions of English irregular verbs that I memorized like poems: go-went-gone; ride-rode-ridden; lie-lay-lain . . . never to be forgotten, together with the correct usage of present perfect and past perfect and the most difficult of all, the verb "to be." How grateful I am that I learned the structure of the language that has become such a tool for writing, for communication through the years. All because of the beautiful Miss Almquist. In a romance that thrilled us, she married the handsome Greek coach but died young of the postwar curse, cancer.

Miss W. was different from the luscious Miss Almquist. Tall, upright, and bespectacled, Miss W. epitomized New England rectitude. She also wore those comfortable American loafers, with plaid skirts, shirts, and cardigans. She taught us what was best in American history, but the one person I remember from her lessons was Abraham Lincoln; she also told us about Louisa May Alcott and I, dreaming and hoping for goodness, thought then that the race problem in America had been solved by President Lincoln.

As the high school years passed, I came to know and admire these American teachers, but it was not a happy time for me. High schools were called *gymnasia*, echoing our ancestors' emphasis on training the body with the mind. Like the public *gymnasia* of the country, it covered the seventh through twelfth years of schooling, but instead of being inside the city, as the public schools were, it was located on an enviable piece of land, on a hill above Thessaloniki's stunning gulf, with a view of Mount Olympos across the water. Those views made Anatolia unforgettable.

In the classroom, I sat by the window and stared at the dark green of the slender cypresses that pointed to a blue sky, their darkness accentuating the softer emerald shades of the sloping hills as they descended to the city, with its patterns of apartment houses and public buildings. The city glistened white in the morning sun, distance hiding all urban ugliness while urging my gaze to skip to the sea—the Thermaic Gulf with its deep waters and secrets without end. And then on to the snow-capped mountain where the gods lived. "You're daydreaming again, Katerina." It's the Ancient Greek hour and the teacher's voice cuts through my escape into beauty, history, and myth. "You're daydreaming again."

Why not? I wanted to talk back to her, but I was a polite child and did not. Yet the words were loud in my head: "You are not teaching me anything exciting. Even Homer becomes a bore, a song without a melody—*Andra mi enepe, Mousa, polytropon.* Analyze each word, learn the Homeric Greek as if it were a puzzle, keep its secrets hidden, keep the stories buried under tedium, ignore the horror of war it depicts, miss out on the irony. What a waste, even to a girl like me who loved language with a passion. Most of the day's subjects followed the same boring pattern.

But how I loved our music class! We walked across the road from the girls' to the boys' school for the after-school chorus rehearsal, a group of us girls ready to join some men from the faculty who sang tenor and bass; I can't remember that any of the school boys joined us. But that one year, two tall, handsome sons of a teacher from Minnesota sang with us. I never learned their names, never had the courage to talk to them. I remember one of them blushed furiously when anyone addressed him. He had blond curls that fell on his forehead. I was in love with men who sang—tenors and basses together. I was in love with singing in chorus, with the harmony that arose and blended and filled me with a joy that led to tears. I watched the young men as they sang, and they became beautiful.

"We gather together to ask the Lord's blessing; He chastens and hastens his will to make known . . . .," we sang. I understood the first sentence. The rest was a mystery, and the history behind the Thanksgiving hymn was still buried in myths told by Americans to themselves. These were the same Americans who believed that they had come to us, sad but proud Greeks, to save us from ourselves. They were good people, those Americans who sang with us. They had come to Greece after the civil war as Fulbright scholars, eager to teach and to share the unique culture that was America. They came to us who as children had known nothing but war; they were innocent people from a land that had not suffered war, and our favorite generalization for them was *aphêlés*—innocent and naïve. I still hear that Thanksgiving hymn we sang in chorus and something inside me bends and loses historical knowledge and the cynicism of years and melts into the words and the melody. *We gather together.* . . . We who are still alive after having seen so much and having learned so much, having hoped so much and having lost all hope. We gather together to remember all those we have lost through the years and all the innocence that was America, now also lost forever.

I find myself again a teen but without the carelessness of young years, a very serious child, in that upper room of Macedonia Hall, the large hall that had a special smell like the wood of an old grand piano. We stand in a semicircle following the directing hands of dear Warren Benson, his very blond, very straight hair falling on his brow, his glasses perpetually low on the bridge of his nose, his overbite with the attractive lisp as he speaks the words, his smile that knows the secrets of music. Benson, who conquered polio as a child, who arrived in Thessaloniki with his serious limp and lovely wife, who would change my life forever and who would become a recognized American composer.

Because during the Nazi occupation from April 1941 to the end of 1944, the school had served as the headquarters of the German command for the Balkans, we held chapel every morning in a building that had been a military barracks. The sun's rays streamed from the east as we stood to sing, "Fairest Lord Jesus, ruler of all nations," led by Miss Ingle, a former missionary, a remarkable woman who was feared and respected, who served as our dean. The irony of the words "ruler of all nations," sung in those German-built barracks by girls who had no idea what they were singing, didn't seem to strike her or us as incongruous. That particular hymn still makes me deeply, unfathomably, sad. While I sang those words, that first month at Anatolia, my mother was dying at home.

By the beginning of my sophomore year a new classroom building had arisen across the road from the main campus, and the girls' school now had a legitimate location. We were not aware that there were tunnels under the school grounds, dug by the Germans for their own protection. We were trying to forget the war. During the mid-day break, together with my best friend, Angela, I noticed the coming of spring in the tender green of the new leaves on the elegant poplar trees, the white aromatic blossoms of the spirea, the darker green of the cypresses. She and I talked about the appealing sound of English words, like the adjective "lovely." She talked about finding our biology teacher—a very tall, angular, and thickly bespectacled American with a deep voice—sexy. She was obviously much more mature than I because I still preferred to daydream of good-looking boys; she was already attracted by the mind rather than the looks. We competed on who would write the best essays since we were the ablest creative writers in the class, but I knew that Angela was smarter than I because she was also gifted in the sciences and I was not. And I was miserable in math.

I disliked the phys. ed. teacher, and the feeling was mutual. I learned this when she told me to wipe that look off my face; I was not aware of any look, much less one that was offensive. It hurt me to the core until a few years later I read C. S. Lewis's *Surprised by Joy*; he described a similar experience with a teacher, and only then was I comforted.

I remember certain afternoons when I would stand on the hill to take in the view that changed constantly, thrilling the senses. I saw the sun's rays break through the clouds over the Thermaic Gulf to strike the waters with silver, and the beauty was so intense that I wept. I didn't know what was happening to me. No one those days talked of teenage angst and of hormones. Again, those tears were redeemed only when I read in Lewis's autobiography that these moments of beauty and emotion were intimations of the Divine.

A couple of my girlfriends were much more aware of boys than Angela and I. We tended to focus on words, and I was also passionate about music. It was during those days, when I was fourteen but felt much older, that boys started noticing me and I received love letters and burning looks from them. All that flattered me but also embarrassed me and made me very uncomfortable. Since most of the boys in my church were related to me or had grown up with me, this strange new sensation had to come from elsewhere. At that time we Free Evangelicals started combining choirs with our Presbyterian friends. Their choir was much larger than ours and the members more mature. Instead of fourteen and sixteen years old, they were eighteen and over. Those were the years when it was perfectly natural for girls to be courted by young men, not boys. The generation before us, having lived in the misery of war and having lost so many men, left the women looking for a spouse to protect and support them. We knew no mothers who worked outside the home. But my generation, barely free of war, hunger, and extreme poverty, dared to think beyond survival, longing for higher education; women were now going to university in Thessaloniki. The theater had opened again and some fine musicians were coming to perform for us, the poor people of Thessaloniki. Gina Bachauer, a Greek pianist who had escaped the extermination of the Jews of Thessaloniki, played one night, and I was transformed. Years later I would go backstage to meet her after a performance in Fayetteville, NC, and I told her how I first heard her when I was a fourteen-year-old in Thessaloniki. I still have a photograph signed by her. I have never since asked for anyone else's photograph or autograph. She remains the only one.

I fancied myself in love with brooding Beethoven. So, when a young man from the Presbyterian choir asked me to go to his home to listen to his new albums, I accepted. His mother was somewhere in the house, but we sat in a room with his record player and he talked about music. I remember very little else about our conversations, and I cannot recall how often I went to his home after school.

My first love had nothing to do with sex but everything to do with music. He was a young man in his early twenties and I was a teen, but that was only natural in Greece during those years, when most men were at least a decade older than their wives.

Yet, I was not thinking of marriage or the future. I was a lonely girl with strange thoughts and worries. My dreams seemed so different from those of the girls around me. In addition to my love for Beethoven, I thrilled at the love between Marie Curie and Peter in that cold lab of theirs in Paris and I had fallen, utterly lost and filled with longing, into the pages of *Pride and Prejudice* and *Rebecca*. I sang Schubert's saddest lieder and even responded to the half-mad religiosity of Dostoyevsky. My girlfriends and I talked about handsome men and exchanged glances with them from a distance, but I never asked the girls for any details and I never revealed to anyone my visits to my friend's house.

Something new and strange was awakening within me, but it had very little to do with my body. I had hidden the love letters, but they had been found by my derisive brother, and all I felt was embarrassment about the emotions expressed in them. But the music lover was a friend, and I was sharing something good with him, though I remember nothing of our conversations—only the music. I did feel the excitement of having a friendship all my own, something secret and definitely aesthetic.

He visited our home also and brought me sheet music to play—the *Souvenir* of Drdla, Weber's *Invitation to the Dance*, and Schubert's oh-so-emotive *Serenade* are still in my possession. When I played the piano in company, he would ask everyone to stop talking because it was "sacrilegious to talk" while I played. How long our special friendship lasted I don't really remember as I, then, could not begin to understand what it was that he felt. I was flattered, and I enjoyed his musical offerings. Then, one day, he told me that he loved me, that he would wait for me to finish school and then he'd marry me, and when we said goodbye, instead of shaking hands as we had done in the past, he kissed me on the lips, and that stunned me so profoundly that I never went to his house again. It was at that moment that I realized to my astonishment that I had never seen my parents kiss each other on the lips in our presence. Our lives had been so sheltered that I had not been to the cinema, and books like those of Jane Austen's, though full of Eros, were not erotic. The kiss shook me profoundly. When I left to study in America, I didn't even say goodbye to him, though later we resumed our friendship.

Anatolia brought something different to our drab postwar lives—extracurricular activities, weird new words and experiences unknown to Greek educational institutions. We learned to say "clubs," though we had no idea what they were. And because they were an addition to the difficult curriculum demanded by the Greek state, our school days were very long. There was very little time left at home. At the beginning we had classes even on Saturday mornings. School, music practice, choir, and church were the only realities of my Greek teenage years.

Teenage Angst

The senses ached. I was sick with desire;
that sickness better than health.

— C. S. Lewis, *Surprised by Joy*

I was now fifteen years old and I was losing interest in my studies and in everything that used to attract me. My favorite music teacher had left the school to return to America together with his lovely wife and their first child, who would not survive surgery in the States. Most of the Fulbright teachers stayed for just two years, so only our Greek teachers and the administrators remained the same. My girlfriends, not constrained by the strict negativity of our evangelical church, went to dances and to the cinema and talked of their exciting life outside school. I could not participate, so they thought me weird; I was beginning to suspect they were right. Family, school, and church were my life, but I was getting bored. I didn't like myself, my body, my surroundings. My grades started slipping. I had been involved in theater, even writing my own play that was produced at school—a truly awful, didactic play. Theater excited me, but that too was forbidden us unless it was moralistic. I heard my friends talking about Tyrone Power, Rita Hayworth, Louis Jourdan, and so many others, and I followed their discussions with envy. I knew what these famous Hollywood personalities looked like because the newspapers, which we devoured, were full of their photos and their images were magnified on the marquees of the many cinemas of the city. In the summertime, in Aristotelous

Square, there was a huge outdoor cinema, so we too could hear the actors' voices and even get a glimpse of the upper half of their images on the lit screens as we, unable to enter, walked around the enclosure. Popular music, filled with Eros, played on the radio, so we too knew the melodies and the words. Fox trot and tango rhythms pulsated all around us. It was a culture we glimpsed but never entered. "We are in the world but not of the world," Daddy would pronounce. And I drifted more and more into a kind of strange melancholic state, unaware that ennui and even angst were part of those dangerous years.

What am I doing? Where is the meaning in all this? Why am I so sad? Ontological questions troubled me. The church and the family gave me scripted answers but they did not always satisfy. I was aware that we were no longer living under occupation and the thought made me giddy. But what was it that was missing? I dreamt of becoming a writer, but most of my life passed in daydreams.

On that particular afternoon I was sitting on the bus, staring at the familiar parts of the city passing by my eyes. I recognize now that I remember that one ride because of what came later. If I had known then that there was such a thing as depression, I would have given my emotional state a name. We passed under the Kamára, the famous Arch of Galerius, the second most distinctive landmark of the city. I looked at those carvings of the Romans in their frozen immobility and I thought, *Once they lived here for a while,* and I felt terribly sad. *St. Paul walked here once, on this Via Egnatia, but I cannot imagine him. Everything is passing.* I quoted Heraclitus to myself: *Ta panta rhei.* A singular verb with a plural noun. One of those rare, strange grammatical constructions we were learning. Everything flows (like a river); everything changes. What about my life? I walked home slowly, not liking myself. The nasty man who almost always followed me home was behind me murmuring the demented refrain of his sick mind. As was my custom I pretended not to hear him, not to see him. We didn't know enough to report him to the police. Who would have listened to us?

Carrying my heavy satchel, I climbed the two flights of stairs, but before I arrived at our landing the door opened and my new mother smiled at me, my older sister directly behind her looking intently at me. "What has happened?" I asked.

"Do you feel something new, something strange is about to happen?" one of them asked.

I was mystified. "What are you talking about?" I could tell that they had a secret; they had been told not to divulge it, but they couldn't help themselves—they wanted to blurt it out. I was reading their expressions very clearly, something fluttering inside me.

"Your Daddy told us to wait for him," Mother said, but I could tell that she would not succeed. Shall I pressure her? Shall I wait? I remained quiet and that worked.

"Your father heard from Mr. Benson."

"Really? How strange. Why would Mr. Benson write to Baba?"

"Well, apparently, he is offering you a scholarship."

At that moment I remembered a conversation with my dear music teacher. I had performed as a traditional one-woman chorus when he approached me. "Would you like to study music in America?"

And I had said, "Yes. I think so. But any kind of professional work will be forbidden me. You have met my father. He would not allow me to go on the stage." I said all this not knowing what one did with a professional music degree. I saw again his regretful smile and I wondered on that afternoon, when I had returned home so sad, whether it was possible that something new could enter my life. Maybe, I hoped suddenly, maybe, I will not be bored all the time.

The Corinth Canal. Nero tried to have the isthmus dug with pick axes but failed. The canal, built at the end of the 19th century, connects the Gulf of Corinth to the Saronic Gulf. Author's photograph.

That evening, Daddy said: "I am going to show you a letter. I don't want to, but I promised your Miss Ingle that I would. It was written by Mr. Benson to Miss Ingle."

"Why are you in possession of a letter addressed to Miss Ingle?"

And I had a vision of the formidable dean riding the bus into the city and walking those commercial blocks filled with loud Greeks— my dean walking to my father's store! How did she find it? What did she think when she heard those uncouth shoemakers arguing prices with my father?

"She had to wait," Daddy said, "because I happened to be busy. She waited very patiently until I finished, and that surprised me. She asked me to read the letter and not to make a decision before I talked to you and to the whole family." He was very hesitant when he handed me the air letter. It was on one sheet of paper that served both as letter and envelope—another one of those ingenious American inventions.

Benson wrote about schools in the south being easier than those in the north and I thought for a moment he was writing about South America. What could I possible study there? Didn't they speak Spanish? I was confused. I read it again. It was simple and straightforward. The college students were offering part of their tuition as scholarship to foreign students, and a Korean girl and I had been chosen. The schools in the south were not as demanding as the schools in the north, he wrote, and even though I had two more years before graduation, I had enough credits to enter Mars Hill Junior College. Mars Hill: *Areos Pagos*, *Areópagos* in demotic Greek, the ancient supreme court of the Athenian city-state. How appropriate. An omen?

"I gave it back to her, immediately," Daddy said as the rest of the family stared at me to see my reaction. "But Miss Ingle insisted that I should ask you first, that I should not keep this a secret." He sounded miserable.

We were quiet for a few minutes and then my brother erupted. "You cannot let her go. You'll regret it. She'll fall in love with some American and never return."

My head started hurting. "Please, let's stop," I begged. "I need to think."

That night Daddy said, "I have no intention of letting you go. But I do need to ask this question: If I let you, would you go?"

"Yes," I said, and I was astonished by my own answer. I was no longer bored, but something that felt like fear landed in my stomach, together with a new giddiness.

That night I dreamt of snow and a horse-drawn carriage and I heard sleigh bells. That's all I knew about America. And the sound of the spirituals sung by the Robert Shaw Chorale. I didn't know then that his singers were white.

The next day the arguments continued. I kept thinking how nice it would be to escape the phys. ed. teacher who had told me to wipe that look off my face, how surprised my classmates would be.

I was only in the fourth form, or tenth grade, as it would be in the American school system. My English had improved tremendously. Benson and his wife would be in the same college and they would be like family. I said to my father, "Babá, you always talk about God's will. You know that in order to travel I would have to apply for a Fulbright grant. Let's pray then and leave it to God's will. If I get the grant, you will have to let me go. If I don't get the grant, I will never bring it up again." And to his later regret, my father agreed.

I continued going to school, my secret kept from my friends and teachers. When I needed to, I walked alone to the American consulate housed in a beautiful building on the waterfront of the city. Only rich Greeks and foreigners lived on that street. I filled out applications and answered "no" when I was asked again and again about any affiliation with the Communist Party. *No, of course not, I had never been a member, I had never been in prison, I had never committed any crime.* I found the questions preposterous. I was only sixteen.

The Angels to Guard Me

We are not orphans cast out into a meaningless void.

—from a lecture by the late Verna Dozier,
Episcopal theologian

I received the Fulbright travel grant, but the arguments at home continued. "You know," Maria, the new mother, told me, "because I am your stepmother everyone will say that I caused you to leave. I want what is best for you, even if they talk badly about me." We were leaning on our elbows, on the front windowsill, looking down at the street and the people across who were opening their shutters after the siesta.

"Thank you," I said to her, knowing that she was an ally. "I love you for it." How familiar the street was, how homely. If I left, would I ever see it again? Would anything ever be the same?

She continued. "Your father told me that your own mother wanted you to get an education. She considered you the smartest of her children."

I didn't let her finish. "Really? I never knew that."

That night my father said, "I know you want an education. I no longer have the money to make it possible for you. I am saying yes for your sake, though I know I will regret it."

My brother remained furious. My older sister and her new fiancé were both regretful but supportive, while my younger sister clung to me as the months passed, pulling us inexorably toward the summer of 1953.

Marilyn Monroe was in the papers and everyone talked of her and Joe DiMagio. "He's so ugly," we said to each other, not knowing anything about American baseball heroes. "How can this beauty be attracted to him?"

Edmund Hillary conquered Mount Everest. We talked of him with astonishment. Stalin died in Russia—what a relief. In England a young Elizabeth was crowned queen. In the Ionian Sea, on the west of our mainland, a terrible earthquake devastated its fabled, beautiful islands. Something seemed to break inside me, and I became sicker and sicker in my body as the time of my departure approached. "Maybe that's a sign," my brother said. "Maybe someone is telling you that you are mad to be going to America." I too suspected so at times, but I had made a decision and would not alter it. I would leave. I was so proud of my steadfastness.

In early August, my dear stepmother went on ahead to her family in Athens. She would be there to see me off. I climbed the hill to my grandfather's house, my heart heavy. Grandmother was her quiet self, but I sensed her sadness and disapproval. My grandfather laid his hand on my head and gave me his blessing. I wept as he prayed, even though I didn't suspect that I would never see them again.

On the last night, my father gathered us in the living room and read the Ninety-First Psalm aloud: "You will not fear the terror of the night," and I remembered all those nights during the war and his reassuring voice quoting this powerful line. Then came the words that I would repeat to myself in future days, months, and years:

For he will command his angels
concerning you
to guard you in all your ways.

On their hands they will bear

you up,

so that you will not dash your

foot against a stone.

(Psalm 91:11–12)

The next morning, we rode a taxi to the port. I was allowed only two suitcases and thirty dollars, a supposedly decent amount in 1953. The ship pulled away from the waterfront, and I looked down to see how the dark water was widening between us. When I dared to look up, I saw only my father's and older sister's sad faces. She waved a handkerchief, trying to stop her tears, while my father raised his fist in the sign of courage. *Kouráyio*, he kept crying, *kouráyio*. I think he needed it more than I. I don't remember who met me at the port of Piraeus. At my step-grandparents' house, their two handsome sons and the long-engaged younger daughter still lived. Feeling fatalistic and foolish, I kept hoping that one of the men would fall in love with me, forcing me to stay in Greece. Everyone seemed sad and confused about my going away, and I agreed that I was a little mad. But days pass, as they do, and now I was on my way to the port again, with a huge emptiness in my belly.

I managed to say goodbye without crying and I sat on the deck of the old, small boat that would take me to Brindisi. There were two other Greek girls traveling on the Fulbright grant, but they were from Athens and a few years older than I. The Corinthian canal was navigable again after the Germans' scorched-earth retreat had made it impassable for four years.

I watched as a tiny pilot ship pulled our larger passenger boat through the canal, the walls on either side impossibly tall and rough, their war scars still visible. The four-mile slow pull through the deep waters filled me with fascination and I lost the focus on my grief for a while. As we emerged into the Corinthian Gulf to make our slow way to the Ionian and the Adriatic Seas, the weather changed. In the Adriatic, the waves reached the deck and the sounds of people getting violently sick surrounded me. Indifferent, I continued pretending to read my book.

It was night when we reached Brindisi on the heel of the Italian boot. I have blocked all the chaos of that night except for one image: me, at the dark entrance of a dark hotel lobby that looks more like the floor of a warehouse, sitting on my suitcases and weeping helplessly. Where we slept and how we got to the train station the following morning remain in a shrouded memory that I haven't tried to unveil. The next day, the train, crossing the leg of Italy toward Naples, was loud and shaky, with passing visions of green light and shadow. It took us most of the day to arrive, and only the stub of that train ticket still in my possession gives reality to an experience I can't quite recall. In the long days of August, it was still light when we boarded the enormous floating city berthed at the port of Naples, an ocean liner named the SS *Independence*. Later I would ask: *Independence from whom, from what?* But I was told that it was not a concept, it was a place—the birthplace of President Truman. Climbing that plank to the second class deck, or club, as they called it, where we Fulbright grantees were relegated, was the worst walk of my young life. I entered a place of luxury and noise, of pretty, arrogant, and self-assured American youth—I, the poorly dressed Greek girl who had known nothing but the poverty of the war years and the limited resources of the aftermath of a civil war.

I prayed: *What have I done? What have I done? Oh, God, make these two years pass fast. I will go home again, never to leave. Forgive my pride.* I remembered my father's insistence that we're in the world but not of the world, words I had resented at times. *So this is what the world is like. I don't like it. It was the sin of pride that brought me to this terrible loneliness in the midst of so many alien people.*

Our cabin had no porthole. It was a large room, which I remember painted in mauve, the lighting soft and indirect. We Greek girls had three of the bunks. The fourth was occupied by a young, pert Jewish-American girl who exuded superiority and irritating self-confidence. Our steward was a patient and kind Black man, my first acquaintance with an African American.

I was in utter misery. I wept the whole time. I think it was on day two that we stopped at the northern city of Genoa and were allowed several hours of exploration. Why I stopped crying and regretting my decision to leave home the moment my feet touched land again I have never understood. But it happened—almost miraculously. I stopped a state of self-pity to enter a new world of interest: in others, in new cities, in new experiences.

Why the guide took us to the Staglieno Cemetery of Genoa instead of to the city itself is another mystery. I remember walking with a group of fellow passengers and listening to the guide as he led us through paths flanked by magnificent statuary. There was one of a tiny old woman at the entrance of a mausoleum. He told us with undisguised pride that this woman had lived a poor life in order to save every penny for her tomb and statue. I found it bizarre beyond words but kept it to myself. Being a Protestant meant that after death nothing on earth mattered. Why waste a lifetime's work on a monument? I pondered this as we returned to our floating luxury and my new world of paying attention.

The deck was crowded with young men and women who intimidated me. I longed to be that carefree, to be confident enough to wear a bathing suit in front of strangers, to chat freely and loudly as they did, maybe even to squeal as the girls did when they dived in the pool. But I did not. Nothing felt free about me.

At Gibraltar the huge ship paused so that vendors in their tiny boats could rush to us with their colorful, useless wares. It was like a painting that had suddenly come alive. I let my eyes feast on the colors and the movement because soon there would be no land to rest the eyes on but long days and nights on the unfamiliar and dangerous waters of the Atlantic Ocean. I kept writing letters.

One pretty and sweet young woman befriended me and asked me if I wanted a Coca-Cola. I had never heard of the drink before. She had blonde curly hair and a huge smile. She was from the Midwest and I came to think of her as the best America had to offer. One of the men who was curious about our various destinations said, when he learned I was going to North Carolina: "They eat grits there." Such scant memories from a long voyage. As Manhattan appeared in the horizon, my pretty young friend pointed out to me landmarks of the island. The one great surprise was that there were so many church steeples rising in the distance.

I dreaded the arrival. What awaited me on shore? Would there be anyone to meet me? In that age of letter writing I had failed to communicate sufficiently with Mr. Benson. Would he come to meet me? I had no idea what the distances were between states.

There was a pleasant official who told us that after we disembarked we would find our luggage under our last name's initial. They probably asked us many questions, but I have no recall of my answers. I was stunned, moving as if in a programmed nightmare that propels but never arrives. In that throng of strangers, I went to stand under the huge letter K hanging from a metal rafter. I found my two battered leather suitcases and I was standing there, lost, not daring to move. Travelers were passing by me, grabbing each other and their suitcases with laughter and what appeared to be joy. How long did I wait? I was getting frightened that I would be left in that alien place all alone when a voice asked: "Are you Katy? Katy Katsarka?" A thrill went through me. *Someone knows my name in this strange land. I am being called by NAME.* Trembling with hope, I turned. There stood a lovely woman with blonde-reddish hair and a tall, dark-haired man with a mustache. I didn't know them, but they were smiling kindly, looking at me.

"Yes," I said, "yes, I am Katy Katsarka."

"Whitey sent us," one of them said and, seeing my confusion, they rushed to explain. "We are friends of Warren Benson. Lois and Bob Roberts. We call him Whitey because of his very light hair."

"Oh!" I wanted to fall in their arms, to tell them of my relief, to thank them for saving me from that total unknowing of arriving in a strange land, to rejoice in being called by name. But necessity took over and they led me away to this new strange life that was just beginning. Lois would take me home with her to Long Island and Bob would go to the heart of New York City and the Radio City Music Hall, where he was first trumpet.

The drive to Long Island in the car was swift, the wind blowing nothing but hot air through the windows. We arrived at their small house, and Lois showed me the bed where I would sleep and the shower in the small bathroom. Something called a television was playing silently in the living room. In the shower now, as the welcomed water poured over me, I saw with dismay how badly my skin had burned on my arms, from my short-sleeve line down; my legs from the knees down were blistering, and in the mirror I saw that my face was turning a wild, red-brown shade. It had been so cool on the ship's deck. How did I burn so badly? The almond smell of Jergen's lotion brings back that first and last serious sunburn of my life, and of the imposed modesty that kept most of my body covered while liberated young bodies nearby plunged into the pool. I want to weep for that poor lost girl, but I didn't feel sorry for myself on that day. Lois would take me to New York City in the evening, to the Radio City Music Hall.

We rode on Fifth Avenue, and all I could think of was how ugly and impersonal the tall buildings were without any balconies. Weird boxes protruded from many of the closed windows and Lois explained that they were air-conditioners—another American invention. We sat in the cool auditorium of the music hall and I marveled at the dancing women, so tall and beautiful with their identical long legs kicking in unison. The movie that night was one I had just seen on board the ship, the delightful and poignant *Roman Holiday.* Immense longing filled me. The ballet was *Orpheus and Eurydice*, my first hint of what would become an ever-present encounter in my education and American life—allusions to Greek mythology. Backstage, I was introduced to the orchestra members by kind Bob Roberts. I drank it all in.

Letters exchanged between my father and Warren Benson did not reveal that the Bensons would leave Mars Hill two days after my arrival.

Toward a New Life

As you set out for Ithaka,
hope your road is a long one,
full of adventure, full of discovery. . .

—C. P. Cavafy, *Ithaka*

The next morning I was scheduled to fly to North Carolina. I had been on the sea many times, and had traveled in trains that covered us with soot, and on many pathetic buses, but I had never before flown on an airplane. LaGuardia Airport gave me vision overload when I saw its parking lot filled with cars. The enormity of their number below me made me dizzy. The sun struck their roofs, rows upon rows of glistening steel. So this is America. Nothing pretty about it. I thanked Lois, knowing that I would never forget her kindness, as I would not forget her husband's help. I climbed onto the plane and sat by a window.

The plane lifted up to land quite soon at the Pittsburgh airport—I have no idea why. I do remember that the attendant was very kind and she took me to a room full of pilots and other airport personnel to wait for the next flight. They asked me questions, and I answered. The skies were indeed friendly those days. Then on to another plane headed for Asheville. A storm darkened the skies, rain hit us mercilessly, and lightning flashed every few seconds. "If we get struck by lightning, will the plane crash?" I asked this of the man in the next seat and he tried to reassure me, but I didn't care. I had left home, I was all alone, and if died, I died. But that assurance that had filled me when my father read the Ninety-First Psalm continued. God's angels would bear me up lest I dash my foot against a stone. And they did.

The plane landed at the tiny Asheville airport and Benson was there to meet me. How kind he was; how lovely to see a familiar face. I told him of his wonderful friends, the Roberts, and their immense kindness to me. He drove on the old mountain road toward Mars Hill College, a two-lane, twisting narrow road, but Benson bragged on its construction. "You notice how it dips on the curves to make turning easier and safer? We have wonderful engineers in America." And somewhere on the way he stopped to show me the marvels of the American supermarket. For some reason the road passed by Grove Park Inn, elegant and European-looking amongst the deep green of the trees and for a moment I thought, *This is the only beautiful building I have seen in America thus far.* The college was not far from the airport, but Benson took his time. We were now on the old road, which seemed deserted of cars and people. He looked uncomfortable as he started talking.

"Katy, you know we lost our first little girl, and now we have a healthy new baby. This job at Mars Hill College was a temporary one for me. I know that your father allowed you to come to America thinking that Pat and I would be here to look after you. And I'm sure you know that we meant to do so. But more than anything else I want to be a composer and to support my family. I have just been offered a position in Ithaca College, where I will teach composition." Like Odysseus, I thought, trying to ignore what he was telling me. These Americans can't stay away from Greek names. "We are leaving for New York State in two days," he said, and I turned my face to the window so he could not see my tears. *Poor Mr. Benson. He feels so bad, but he is doing what is right for his family.*

Sixteen-year old freshman ready for class.

"I understand," I whispered.

We arrived at the deserted campus. "Only a small group of students is in residence," he told me. "The rest will be here in ten days. The students who are here are part of an organization called BSU, the Baptist Student Union. They are the leaders of the campus." He stopped the car and got out to greet someone passing by. "This lady will be your piano teacher." An older woman, very old-fashioned in dress, hairdo, and demeanor, stopped to greet us. She had a sweet smile and very kind eyes. "Meet Miss Martha Biggers." We shook hands and she welcomed me.

So this was America? A campus with very few one-to-two-story buildings, several of them quite old, teachers who looked as if they belonged to the last century, one empty street, and a future without the only person I had known in the past. An old clapboard building, white-painted and quaint, was my dormitory, on that one main street of campus. "Mother Fulbright," the housemother, white-haired and a bit stooped over, with loving blue eyes, welcomed me with warmth and showed me to my ugly room, one flight up. There were two single beds in it, and I sat on the one closest to the window. Below it I saw a small amphitheater made of grass and a few stones, and again I remembered the Greeks, whose legacy seemed to be everywhere. "Wherever I go Greece wounds me." I was hurting.

I sat in that room alone as night fell and wrote one of my many letters home, describing everything in glowing terms. No one must know how disappointing it all looked. I sighed. It served me right. Before I slipped into self-pity, someone knocked on the door, and two older girls looked in. They introduced themselves and said, "We are having Bible study and prayer meeting. Would you like to join us?" It was then that I decided all would be well. This was the language of my church and of my family in Greece. No one among my Greek

Orthodox girlfriends would ever have mentioned the Bible and prayers. This language was more familiar than even my native tongue. I was home, for the next two years. Growth and change would come slowly, but they were inevitable. My mind, like a flower bud, would open under the light of knowledge and learning. I didn't know on that night that it would be more than seven years before I would see my family again.

•536•

One of my father's handwritten thousand-page memoir. This page describes the torture of seeing mirages on their night marches. They are seeing phantom city streets.

RECOMMENDED BIBLIOGRAPHY

For those who want to learn more about
the Greek involvement in WWII and the Resistance.

Andrews, Kevin. *The Flight of Icaros*. Penguin Travel Library, 1959.
A travel account by a passionate young Philhellene of his three years
backpacking in the Peloponnesos and elsewhere in Greece during the
most dangerous and fraught time of the civil war. He met with the
wildest Greeks and wrote lovingly of them.

Cavafy, C. P. *Collected Poems*. Translated by Edmund Keeley
and Philip Sherrard. Princeton, N.J. Princeton University Press,
2009.

Christides, Christos. *Chronia Katohis* (Years of Occupation). Athens: 1971. An excellent but painful daily report on the struggles of living under occupation. He has detailed accounts of the *limós* (famine)
and the efforts to keep Greeks from extinction. Only in Greek. The
diary focuses only on life in Athens.

Compton, Carl C. *The Morning Cometh: 45 Years with Anatolia College*. The Board of Trustees of Anatolia College, 2008. A
self-deprecating account of his love affair with Anatolia College
and the Greek people. He served the college for decades but also
worked tirelessly as UNRRA's regional director in Northern Greece
right after the occupation. This edition includes his detailed obser-
vations in letters to his wife about the destruction in the country
he helped rebuild. Available in both Greek and English.

Drez, Ronald J. *Heroes Fight Like Greeks*. Denver: Ghost Road Press, 2009. A rather gushing account of the Greek resistance to Mussolini's Italians.

Electris, Theodore. *Written on the Knee: A Diary from the Greek-Italian Front of WWII*. Translated by his daughter, Helen Electrie Lindsay. Minneapolis: Scarletta Press, 2008. The letters were written by a doctor from Thessaloniki with detailed accounts of the miseries of the front.

Henderson, Mary. *Xenia—A Memoir, Greece 1919–1949*. London: George Weidenfeld & Nicolson Ltd., 1988. The account of a privileged young woman who contributed to the war effort as nurse and journalist. A Greek, she was educated in England. She later married a British diplomat. Very sympathetic to the Greek agony during the war against Mussolini and the occupation, she was less so in writing about the resistance.

Hondros, John Louis. *Occupation Resistance, The Greek Agony*. New York: Pella Publishing Co., 1983. The definitive work on the resistance; meticulously documented, impartial, dispelling the many myths surrounding the resistance. A powerful work.

Keeley, Edmund. *Inventing Pardise*. New York: Farrar, Strauss, and Giroux, 1999. A delightful, pre war journey through Greek literature with Henry Miller, George Seferis, and others. Erudite and poetic.

Mazower, Mark. *Inside Hitler's Greece*. New Haven, Conn.: Yale University Press, London, 1993. A superbly researched and written history of Greece's suffering in WWII. The definitive story of the occupation.

Mazower, Mark, editor. *After the War Was Over. Reconstructing the Family, Nation, and State in Greece, 1943–1960.* Princeton, N.J.: Princeton University Press, 2000. The horrific memories of those involved in the resistance and the injustices that followed.

Myers, E. C. W. *Greek Entanglement.* London: Rupert Hart-Davis, 1955. A detailed recounting of the brigadier's courageous involvement in the Greek mountains, among the partisans of the left and of the right during the tough years of the resistance. Part apologia, not only of his battles with the Greek factions but also as a Special Operations Executive (SOE), of the intractable Foreign Office.

McGrew, William. *Educating across Cultures: Anatolia College in Turkey and Greece.* Rowman and Littlefield, 2015. Dr. McGrew served as president of Anatolia for decades and has written an exhaustive, fascinating history of American missionary zeal in the nineteenth century and the commitment of young missionaries to educating young Armenians and Greeks in Turkey and Greece. Like Dr. Compton's account, this is written with inside knowledge of Anatolia College.

Origo, Iris. *A Chill in the Air, An Italian War Diary, 1939–1940.* New York: New York Review of Books, 2017. One of the privileged Italian women observing her culture changing as Mussolini gains in power and madness.

Powell, Dilys. *An Affair of the Heart.* Athens: Efstasiadis Group S. A., 1994. The wife of an archaeologist, Powell learned to love Greece before the war and returned afterwards to renew friendships with the people who had been involved in the digs.

Psychoundakis, George. *The Cretan Runner: His Story of the German Occupation*. Translated from the Greek by Patrick Leigh Fermor. New York: New York Review Books, 1998. Detailed account of the dangers he encountered as he assisted members of the Special Operations Executive (SOE) in the wild terrain of Crete by a young, uneducated shepherd. A remarkable achievement.

Theotokas, George. *Tetradhia Imerologiou* (Diary Notebooks). Athens, 1939–1953. The daily jottings of an important Greek writer during the turbulent years. In Greek.

Tsatsos, Jeanne. *The Sword's Fierce Edge*. Nashville: Vanderbilt University Press, 1969. Ioanna Tsatsos was sister to the poet Seferis and wife to Greek professor and politician Constantine Tsatsos. Her diary focuses mainly on the pain of famine in Athens and her efforts to combat it.

Wason, Betty. *Miracle in Hellas: The Greeks Fight On*. New York: Macmillan, 1943. Wason was a radio correspondent for CBS. She witnessed the beginning of the occupation, and those eyewitness accounts are quite moving. But she left Greece soon thereafter, and though she wrote during the war, the subsequent reportage has a hearsay feel to it.

Zesiades, Leonidas. *Thessaloniki: What I Remember*. Thessaloniki: Parateretés, 1991. In Greek.

Zesiades, Leonidas. *In Thessaloniki, Then . . .* Thessaloniki: Parateretés, 1995. In Greek. These two delightful memoirs of the Thessaloniki of my childhood were written by the brother of our dearest friend, Dinos Zesiades. They lived near us and Dinos makes an appearance early in my own memoir; later he joined our family.

The most important resource for me is found in my father's ten notebooks, handwritten just for me, of his own life in Adrianople and Thessaloniki, and his memories of the Balkan wars, WWI, Greco-Italian war, and WWII. With gratitude.

The biblical quotes in chapter superscriptions are from the New Revised Standard Version. Other chapter quotes are from C. S. Lewis's autobiography, *Surprised by Joy*. New York: Harcourt, Brace and Company, 1955.

The sea, pine trees, and fishing boats, with hills in the distance. A scene that stays in the mind of those who long for Greece. Author's photograph.

ACKNOWLEDGMENTS

How does one begin to express a lifetime of gratitude? For my patient, longsuffering grandparents and their sacred memory I offer my thanks first, and then for my faithful father and sad mother who died so young. Also, for the generous Maria Demopoulou who became our second mother and a loving support to my father. To my siblings, Doritsa, Kostaki, and Niki, go my love and gratitude for their unfailing love to me even after I left them. To my *ekklesia* in Thessaloniki, to the people who loved me as a child and prayed for me. To my father and grandfather I owe thanks for a faith that has withstood many years of living, of failing, and of metanoia. Because of my family and community, the core of my being has stayed filled with the trust that assures me: God is love. Even though we may no longer agree on biblical interpretation and theology, I am bound to them by the early bonds of faith and hope that are never severed. I am who I am because of them.

I also offer thanks to the members of the Cherokee Round Table in Louisville who listened to the early chapters of this memoir and who first encouraged me to shape them into a book; and to the Valle Crucis Writers in Boone, N. C., who have been with me as friends and coworkers since 2007 and who have also listened to these memories as they visited me. To my late husband who loved my family and admired my Greek background with the passion of a Philhellene and to my children and grandchildren who consider themselves Greek, with pride.

To my friend Nancy Fitzgerald, who served as both editor and publisher; to copyeditor Jen Hackett; to graphic designer Brenda Klinger; and to proofreader Amy Wagner, I offer thanks for their professionalism and for making the fulfillment of a dream possible.

And to the land Elytis called "golden-green leaf drowning in the sea," my unremitting nostalgia.

Made in the USA
Middletown, DE
12 November 2023

42480095R00144